Gone, But Not Forgotten

Messenger Printing, St. Louis, Missouri

ISBN 0-9726006-0-4

Pictured in photo is George Davis Sr., George Davis Jr. and George Davis III.
Photo was taken in 1938.

Dedicated to George Davis , Sr., a man who loved his church and cemetery.

3

Acknowledgments

I owe a debt of gratitude to those who helped me in these long months in the research for this book. Rachel Black, a youth member of Youth In Action was willing to help in the research process. "Thank you for the hundreds of hours in the library researching and all the long hours of rummaging through the boxes of materials." Researching for this book was like trying to put together a puzzle without having the necessary pieces.

Also, thank you to my associates, Angie Carey and Katie Bland, (youth members of Youth In Action) for all their research, typing, and translating. Thanks to Mr. George Davis III for all his photographs, letters, and legal documents. And special gratitude goes to Congressman, Todd Akin, and State Senator, Mike Gibbons, for all their help in obtaining all the military records which made this book possible.

Thanks to John D. Avery for his help in writing *Funeral Practices of the late 1800's & eartly 1900's.* And a big thanks goes to John Beck of Emmis Communications for his financial support in printing portions of this book.

Finally, thank you to my wife, Lisa who supported me throughout this project and helped with the final touches!

Table of Contents

Introduction

As a boy growing up in Kirkwood, I lived on Edna Avenue and attended Osage Elementary School. In 1964-65, I was in the Boy Scouts, working on my photography merit badge and searching for interesting things to photograph. I remembered this old cemetery by the Green Parrot Inn Restaurant, 12200 Old Big Bend at Ballas Road. The old sign said, "Quinette Cemetery Founded 1873". I walked throughout the cemetery looking at all the marble tombstones. I found about eight to fifteen of them. Then, I took out my camera and began taking some interesting pictures of good and bad tombstones. Little did I know this would be an historic walk back in time. I did not know at that time I was going to write a book nor did I wish to. I took all the photos I wanted, and then I put them into a scrapbook and earned my merit badge. I still enjoy photography and love old photos. But now, over 36 years later the tombstones are gone, and only the old photos of the stones remain.

The cemetery sign says it was founded in 1873, but we believe it may date back to 1863 and contain 100 to 200 graves. It is said that many of the people buried in Quinette were Confederate and Union soldiers. The cemetery was a free place of burial for people of African descent, who lived within five miles of the cemetery or anyone else the trustees of the cemetery approved. Quinette Cemetery is listed as an historic cemetery, and is one of five slave burial grounds in the state of Missouri. Much research, experience, and personal interviews with dozens of people will now tell the story, Gone, But Not Forgotten. Mary Broderick Chomeau said it best with her 1965 writings of Quinette Cemetery, "Quinette Cemetery at Ballas and Big Bend Roads, with sheets of newsprint and big crayons to make a rubbing of one of the tombstones in this very old burial ground. The charming wrought-iron picket fence which used to mark its boundaries as well as many of the headstones in the plot have disappeared in recent years, the booty of second-hand dealers and ghouls. But the old cedars, the carpet of myrtle, the yuccas and iris stoutly blooming marked the ground as God's Acre, while the protective wall of Osage Orange trees planted for a western windbreak marked its limits. The earliest graves in this cemetery date back to Civil War times and according to tradition, the plot was first federally owned and used for burial of prisoners of war. There are two small markers with indecipherable lettering, six inches square and about eighteen inches high which resemble military markers."

In this book, there are copies of two rubbings taken from the most prominent of the tombstones remaining in Quinette Cemetery. " It marks the grave of a man who appears in the History of Kirkwood by Mrs. June Dahl as one of the earliest businessmen of the town. Napoleon Morris owned a dram shop. Gus Bopp remembers his masonic funeral when there was a large cortege of marchers from the center of Kirkwood to Quinette accompanied by the Masonic Band. His headstone is reminiscent of monuments in the old cemetery at Ste. Genevieve, Missouri, but the likeness may be due to nothing more than the taste of the era. However, the fact that his name is Napoleon might indicate that he originally came from the French settlement." Another prominent person is Mary Carter, who died about 1900 as a centenarian and is buried in Quinette Cemetery. She came to Kirkwood from Virginia and Wheeling, West Virginia at the end of the Civil War. She was the slave of Mr. and Mrs. John Joliffe Yarnall, the grandparents of Sue Yarnall (Mrs. Harlow P. Donovan). She had one daughter, Jemima, wife of John Martin who worked for a Webster Groves family."

There are four streets in Kirkwood named for early colored residents who are also buried in Quinette. Spears Street is named after Hannah and Sandy Manassa Spears. Bouyer Street was named after Sam and Sophie Bouyer. The street, Whitson was named for Arthur Whitson. Finally, the last street is named for Del Reed.

A Collection of Photographs of Quinette Cemetery taken in 1964-65 by Keith Rawlings working on his Photography Merit Badge for Boy Scouts.

REV. W.M. MARTIN
1836
ALCY HIS WIFE
1832—1912

History of the Families for which the streets are named.

Still alive today is one of the oldest African-Americans in Kirkwood, Bertha Spears Evans, who is 97 years old as of 2002. She can tell you so much history and information about Kirkwood. The following is a culmination of several interviews with her. Sandy Spears was one of the first real estate agents of Meacham Park. Sandy Spears' family was reared on Big Bend Road. Adam Green married Cecelia Spears from Brewton, Escambia County, Alabama. She was a brown skin lady who portrayed the genetic representation of her African, Indian and European heritage. Cecelia was the daughter of a mulatto man who was half Negro and Seminole Indian. Her mother's name was Hannah and her father was Manassa Sandy, Sr. They were the parents of Manassa Sandy Jr. born 1857, Cecilia, born 1860, Alonzo, born 1862, Walter, born 1864, Sarah, born 1866, and Jane born in the 1860's. Sandy Manassa Spears Jr. was a member of the Reorganized Church of Jesus Christ of Latter Day Saints prior to 1860's while living in Brewton, Alabama. According to the oral tradition, Sandy Jr. went to St. Louis, Missouri and stayed with a family named Grangers...Sandy Jr. later sent for his family to come to St. Louis, Missouri to include his father and mother. The family left Alabama with a group of Mormons who were migrating to Independence, Missouri. The Spears family and Adam and his wife Cecelia Spears Green all settled in the area of St. Louis County called Meacham Park, Kirkwood, Missouri. Sandy Spears met a young lady named Sophia Saint James. Her mother was of African, Indian and European descent and her father was French Canadian. Sophia and Sandy Spears Jr. were the parents of Stella, Helen, Sadie, Eugene, Arthur, Allena, Allen, Viola, Bertha, and Oliver Spears. Bertha Spears Evans is living in Kirkwood.

Another street is Bouyer, a short street off the 300 block of South Fillmore. Margaret Johnson Frazier, who worked as a housekeeper for Mr. and Mrs. Lorraine F. Jones Jr., was quoted in the Kirkwood Historical Review, September 1965, with an interesting biography of her grandparents Sam and Sophie Bouyer. "They came from White Chimneys, Virginia, near the Potomac River in 1830 down the Ohio and up to St. Louis by a boat chartered by Judge Joseph Sale, and filled with his family, the slaves and their children. Judge Sale had purchased land next to the John Sappington Estate. The Bouyers had twenty-one children, some of whom died in infancy. Mrs. Frazier remembers Frank Bouyer, a Kirkwood preacher. He is buried in Father Dickson's Cemetery. Some of the other children, Sallie, Linnie, Cloe, Laura, Charlie and John, (twins) are all buried in Quinette. John was a driver for Polar Wave Ice and Fuel Company. Sallie married James Johnson and had eight children, amongst them Mrs. Frazier. Linnie married Levi Madison, one of whose daughters was Rose who became Catholic in her late years, giving as her reason an endearing description, 'I always liked the candles and the bric-a-brac!' Grandmother Sophie Bouyer died in 1911 at the age of 83."

Sophie Bouyer (1828-1911)

A third street, Whitson, which runs from East Clinton and parallel to Fillmore was named for Arthur Whitson who was a mail-clerk at the Post Office Downtown for eighteen years and was President of the first Civic Club amongst the colored group in Kirkwood.

The fourth street is off the 900 block of North Harrison . It is named for Del Reed who owned a drayage business in Kirkwood. Not much information was available for this family.

Gone, But Not Forgotten

The History of Quinette Cemetery

Mr. George Davis, Sr. was a long time member of the AME Church in Kirkwood and was a trustee of the Church and on the clean up committee for the Cemetery. He had a record of conveyance of property from Luke Brockway and wife to William Martin, Henry Nash and George Sleet on June 20th, 1866, recorded in Book 320, page 315 of the 'County Records.' This date substantiates the possibility of Federal beginnings for Quinette as a burial place for soldiers and prisoners of the Civil War.

Also recorded on the same sheet of paper and in the same handwriting is a "quitclaim" deed dated 1873 for the same two acres of land and signed by the trustees, possibly of Olive Chapel, "The men were James Mitchell, John Johnson, Abraham Rice, Kirkey Grey (Uncle of Arthur Whitson), Henry Taylor, James Bowles, John Porter, Willis Mitchell, Abraham Thompsom, Joseph Woodbridge, George Turner, Landry Thompson, Charles Thornton, John Martin, Stuart Anderson, and Andrew Dunn. These men represented Olive Chapel, the African Methodist Episcopal Church which was originally in the three hundred block of West Washington Avenue and is now at 301 South Harrison. This church was founded in 1853 and is amongst the oldest churches in Kirkwood."

Olive Chapel was possibly named after Oliver Quinette who represented the "Quinette Addition"; however, there are several stories about the connection of Olive Chapel and Quinette Cemetery, but the one that makes the most sense is the information on Oliver Quinette according to a letter written by his grandaughter, Adele Quinette Phelps.

"Oliver Quinette (1817-1882) was known as an architect, builder and real estate broker in St. Louis and St. Louis County. Quinette was the name given to a real estate addition

13

west of the city of St. Louis, dedicated February 17, 1859 by Oliver Quinette. The Quinette Road, which was renamed Big Bend Road and later Old Big Bend Road is named after him. The only section that still exists as Quinette Road is off of Big Bend Road in Valley Park. The Cemetery was in this section called Quinette Addition and was on Quinette Road; therefore, it is believed to be named Quinette Cemetery.

Quinette was a stockholder in the Missouri Pacific Railway. He was one of the six men who broke ground for the Railway. He was present on the inaugural run of the railroad to Jefferson City when the cars went off the track and collapsed over the Gasconade River. A number of passengers were killed. Quinette suffered the crippling of a limb as a result of the Gasconade disaster. He died in 1882."

Oliver Quinette

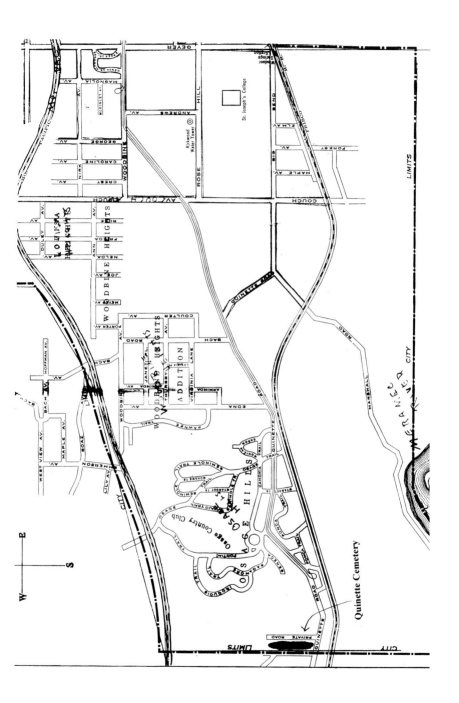

15

The Grave Digger

Richard James, who lives in Rock Hill , now 91 years old, tells the story of his father. Henry James, born in 1885 and died in 1981, is buried in Father Dickson Cemetery. Henry James was a grave digger who dug many graves in Quinette Cemetery, Father Dickson Cemetery and St. Peter's Cemetery. Richard remembers as a boy his father taking him hunting in Quinette Cemetery for rabbits and raccoons. Richard remembers that most folks were buried in pine boxes but some were buried in nothing at all. He said that his father was paid in cash by those who could afford it, otherwise they would give his father food as payment.

Henry James in his garden in the Summer of 1978.

The Family of Bertha Spears Evans

Bertha Spears Evans

Bertha Spears Evans was born in Kirkwood, Missouri in April of 1905 to Sofia St. James Spears (1860-1953) and Sandy Manassa Spears Jr. (1857-1916) who was a real estate agent in Meacham Park. Bertha was the last born of nine children, Stella, Helen, Sadie, Eugene, Arthur, Allena, Allen, Viola, Oliver and Bertha. Bertha says that her family was very blessed because the family never went hungry. They lived and worked on a farm so they had plenty to feed the entire family.

Sandy Manassa Spears Jr. was a member of the Reorganized Church of Jesus Christ of Latter Day Saints prior to 1860's while living in Brewton, Alabama. According to oral tradition, Sandy Jr. went to St. Louis, Missouri and stayed with a family. Sandy later sent for his family to come to St. Louis to include his father and mother, Sandy Manassa Sr. and Hannah Spears. The family left Alabama with a group of Mormons who were migrating to Independence, Missouri. The Spears family decided to settle in the area of St. Louis County called Meacham Park, now Kirkwood, Missouri. Sofia St. James Spears worked at General Grant's Farm for a short while helping out her mother, Harriet Taylor St. James. Harriet Taylor St. James and Shopia's Aunt and Uncle, Matilda and Washington Green are buried in Quinette Cemetery. In her spare time, Sofia would read books and sew quilts.

Bertha attended the little wooden 1st Baptist Church for school through 3rd grade. Next, Bertha attended Booker Washington School on Van Buren. On her way to school everyday, Bertha had to pass the white school just to get to her school. Bertha graduated in 1918 from Booker Washington with a graduating class of 20 students (unheard of for a black institution). After school, Bertha began to teach night sewing classes at Webster University. She would have regular fashion shows that included all of her work. Her future husband designed the programs for the shows. In her spare time, Bertha worked at the School for the Blind.

In July of 1936, Bertha Spears was wed to Harold Evans. The wedding took place outside in a small town in Illinois. It was small and only a few close relatives attended. Bertha and Harold had to keep their marriage a secret because Bertha could get in trouble for having two masters at the same time. Harold and Bertha were unsuccessful at having their own children so they opted to foster two children instead. Therefore, they have no grandchildren.

Bertha has witnessed many changes in Kirkwood first hand. She remembers when the first Ford car drove down Big Bend Road and when the first telephone was available for use. Bertha Spears Evans is the only living child of Sofia and Sandy Spears Jr. She lives in Kirkwood, Missouri and still cooks her own meals in her apartment.

Bertha Spears Evans

Sophia St. James Spears

Mathilda Green

Sandy Manassa Spears

Mother of Meacham Park Resident Prepared Meals For Gen. Grant

Mrs. Sophia St. James Spears is one of the oldest living pioneers of Kirkwood. She was born in Fredericktown, Mo., in 1860 and moved to the city of Kirkwood at the age of three. Mrs. Spears is the mother of ten children, six girls and four boys, Estella Anthony, Sadie Bailey, Allen Spears, Viola Woods, Bertha Evans and Oliver Spears. Four are now deceased. She is a great-grandmother of 12 children. Mrs. Spears lived on Grant's farm before and after he was president. She remembers the 18th president quite well as her mother prepared a great many of his meals. Among her many relics of years passed, she has a sausage grinder that belonged to Gen. Grant.

Mrs. Spears is a great lover of books and artistic needlework. Before her eyes began to fail, she was a reader of many books, and many beautiful quilts were made

by her skilled hands. At the age of 9ß she still has an excellent memory and is an exceptional conversationalist. Mrs. Spears resides at 203 New York St., Meacham Park.

Article printed in a local Meacham Park Community Paper in 1952.

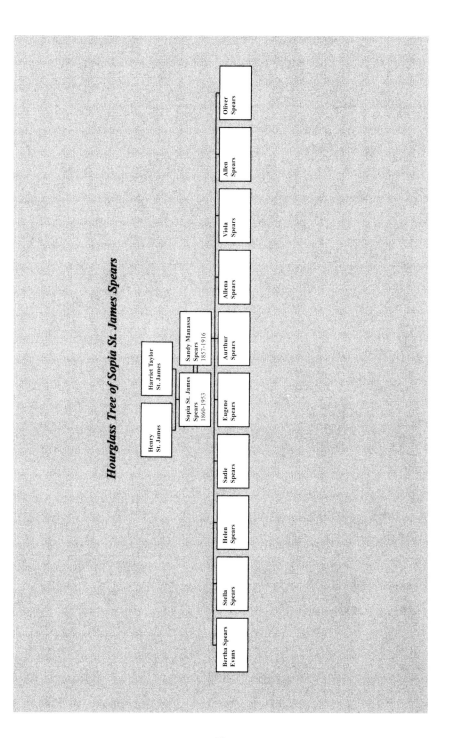

Hourglass Tree of Sopia St. James Spears

Henry St. James

Harriet Taylor St. James

Sopia St. James Spears 1860-1953

Sandy Manassa Spears 1857-1916

Bertha Spears Evans

Stella Spears

Helen Spears

Sadie Spears

Eugene Spears

Aurthur Spears

Allena Spears

Viola Spears

Allen Spears

Oliver Spears

23

The Gray-Whitson Family

Four Generations of Kirkwood Negro
Family Spans over 125 years

Gray-Whitson Family

Contributed by Michael Whitson

First Generation:

Great-grandfather Henry Whitson

Born 1831   Died 1878

Buried in Quinette Cemetery, Big Bend Rd. Kirkwood, MO. Quinette is an old Negro Cemetery given to slaves and free Negroes by the US Government. Henry lived in Kirkwood, worked in Webster Groves. Also later lived in Webster Groves. What is now #69 Gore Ave. across from Walbart Nursery. The house is still standing at that location.

Occupation: Black Smith

Civil War Veteran, Sergeant in Union Army--65 USCT INF Co. F
Enlisted December 20, 1863   Discharged August 15, 1865

Married Louisa Moriah Gray of Kirkwood, MO

Arthur Henry Whitson was born 1878 as a result of this marriage. In 1878 Henry Whitson died. My Great grandmother, Louisa Gray Whitson moved back to Kirkwood with her two brothers. Louisa lived with her brothers and then her son, Arthur until her death in December 1920. She was buried in Father Dickson Cemetery.

Great Uncles:

George Washington Gray and Kirke James Gray resided in what is now known as the 300 block of South Fillmore, Kirkwood, Mo. (1909 map of Kirkwood 4th ward area.) George W. Gray died around 1903, buried in Quinette Cemetery, Big Bend Rd. Kirkwood, Mo.

Kirke James Gray was born in 1857 and died July 4, 1924. He was a minister at the Rose Hill Baptist Church, later known as the 1st Baptist Church. (1909 map of Kirkwood 3rd ward area.) Kirke and wife Maria, charter members building cost $630.00 in 1870; debt free by 1883. The church was located at Railroad St. and Clinton Ave. Kirke was constable of the Bonhomme District during the 1870s. Kirke resided at 300 block of Fillmore Ave. until his death in 1924, buried in Father Dickson Cemetery, Sappington Rd, Crestwood, Mo. Other accomplishments during Kirke's life. Brought his freedom

27

and brother and sister out of slavery! Lillian G Smith, only living granddaughter, 92 years of age, resides in St. Louis, Mo. Born February 2, 1898.

Second Generation:

Grandfather: Arthur Henry Whitson Sr. born in Webster Groves, Mo., May 27, 1878 and died May 17, 1954. He was 75 years old and is buried in Father Dickson Cemetery. Arthur worked as a "Pullman Porter" on the railroad in the early 1900s. He married Daisy Holmes, from Metropolis-Cairo, Ill. who was born on April 2, 1881, and dies June 5, 1973 at age 92. Arthur resided in Kirkwood for 49 years at the same residence in the 400 block of South Fillmore. He married in 1903 and was married for 51 years. Daisy's occupation: Housewife, and property manager. Arthur's occupation: Postal Clerk, "Special Clerk" at the Old Post Office at 815 Olive, St. Louis, Mo. from 1903-1947 (44 years of service).

In 1934, the city of Kirkwood dedicated "Whitson Street" in honor of the Whitson family, for community services in behalf of the neighborhood home owners and residents of Kirkwood over 65 years. A sum of $10.00 was paid for the usage of the Whitson name!

Third Generation:

Uncle Lawrence Henry Whitson was born in Kirkwood, Mo., September 22, 1904 (342 S. Fillmore). He died October 25, 1961 in St. Louis County Hospital (age 57) and is buried in Father Dickson Cemetery. He was raised in Kirkwood , and attended Booker T. Washington Elementary School. He moved to the "Ville" area in St. Louis, Mo. and attended Phyllis Wheatly School, then attended Charles Sumner High School and graduated with the class of 1922. (Charles Sumner High School is the oldest Negro high school west of the Mississippi.)

Pictured above is the gravestone of Henry Whitson. This gravestone can no longer be found in Quinette Cemetery. This Photograph was taken 1964-1965.

The Mitchell Family

The Mitchell Family

James Anderson Mitchell was born in 1856 and died in the 1920's. He was the Grandfather of George Davis, Jr. He worked as a Porter on the Missouri-Pacific Railroad and as a Shoemaker for International Shoe Company. James also became a 33rd degree Mason. He was married to Medea Houston on October 15, 1884. James Anderson Mitchell is buried in Quinette Cemetery.

Medea Cornelia Houston Mitchell was the Daughter of Robert and Martha Parker Houston of St. James Missouri. Medea Houston Mitchell is buried in Quinette Cemetery.

Willis Mitchell, brother of James Anderson Mitchell, was born in 1847 and was emancipated in 1863. Willis Mitchell lived in Kirkwood and is buried in Quinette Cemetery. {See Blacks in the Military for Willis Mitchell's Service Records.}

James Anderson Mitchell   Medea Cornelia Houston Mitchell

This License authorizes any Judge, Justice of the Peace, licensed or ordained Preacher of the Gospel, or any other person authorized under the laws of this State, to solemnize Marriage between *James A. Mitchell*, of *Kirkwood*, County of *St. Louis*, and State of *Missouri*, who is *over* the age of twenty-one years, and *Media Houston*, of *Kirkwood*, County of *St. Louis*, and State of *Missouri*, who is *over* the age of eighteen years.

Witness my hand as Recorder, with the seal of Office hereto fixed, at my Office in Clayton, the *Fifteenth* day of *October* 1884

By *D. Sch---* DEPUTY *F. Ruehl* RECORDER

STATE OF MISSOURI, } ss.
COUNTY OF ST. LOUIS.

This is to Certify, that the undersigned *is a minister of the Gospel* did, at *Kirkwood* in said County, on the *above* day of *Oct 15th* A. D., 1884, unite in Marriage the above named persons.

Frederick McKinney Pastor of Second Baptist Church of Kirkwood

The Marriage License of James Anderson Mitchell and Medea Cornelia Houston Mitchell
October 15, 1884

34

The following is the printed copy of the handwritten statement by James A. Mitchell regarding his family history.

I James A Mitchell was the youngest son of James and Nancy Mitchell. There were nine children in our family; seven boys and two girls. My father belonged to the family of Jessie Benton on a farm down in Knoxville, Tennessee. He came to St. Louis as the valet of Senator Thomas H Benton. Jessie Benton died and as the property and slaves had to be divided my father was sold south to allow his youngest brother to stay with his parents; my father begged to be allowed to be sold instead and he was sold south. My father's mother was a full blooded African dissidence her father being a chief of what tribe I do not know only I have often heard my father speak about the silver half moon she always wore around her neck representing what tribe she belonged to. The slave owners never liken' this emblem anyway for her. After the war broke out in 1863, father brought his family and came to St. Louis. The duel between Thomas H Benton and Jim Lucas on Blondy Island my father being valet was wounded by a wild bullet from Lucas' gun. He always limped from this wound. We came to St. Louis August 8, 1863 from Helena, Arkansas. Born September 1856.

My mother was mixed dissent Scotch, Irish, Indian, and Negro. She always used the name of Wiley as that is the family she belonged to. Her father was a Scotch Irish man.

Jessie Knoxville Tennessee
Big plantation Thomas Howard no slaves

Tally sheet used by James A. Mitchell as clerk for his neighbor Dr. John Pittman.

PROGRESSIVE CITY TICKET

Tuesday, April 3, 1900.

For Mayor, ╫
W. M. Daly.   74

For Marshal,
Columbus Strohm. ╫64

For Collector,
Gerard DeHoog. ╫73

For Police Judge,
Hugo S. Jacobi.   76

For Aldermen—4th Ward,
M. W. Cronin. ╫ 72
Fred Heege.   ╫72

The following is a handwritten statement by James Anderson Mitchell regarding his family history.

family seven girls and two boys
my fathers belonged to the family
of Bentons on a farm down in
Knoxville Tenn. He came to St.
Louis as the valet of Thomas H. Benton
Jessie Benton died and as the property
and slaves had to be divided my
father was sold south. To allow
his youngest brother to stay with his
parents my father begged to be
allowed to be sold in stead and he
was sold south. My fathers mother
was a full-blooded African Princess
her father being a chief of what
tribe I do not know only I have often
heard my father speak about the
silver half moon she always wore
suspended around her neck
representing what tribe she
belonged to. The slave owners
never taken this emblem away from
her. After the war broke out
in 1863 father brought his family
& came to St Louis. The duel
between Thomas H. Benton & Jim
Lucas on Bloody Island my
father being a lad was wounded by
a wild ballet from Lucas gun
He always limped from this wound
We came to Aug 8, 1863 from
Helena Arkansas, Born Sept
1856

my mother was of mixed descent
Scotch Irish Indian + Negro. She used
the name of Wiley as that is the family
she belonged to, her father was a
Scotch Irish man

Jessie Knoxville Tenn
big plantation   Thomas H. owned no slaves

36

James Anderson Mitchell, grandfather of George C. Davis Jr.
Mitchell was born in 1856 and became a 33rd-degree Mason.

Willie Mitchell

Willis Mitchell's Discharge Papers from the Military.

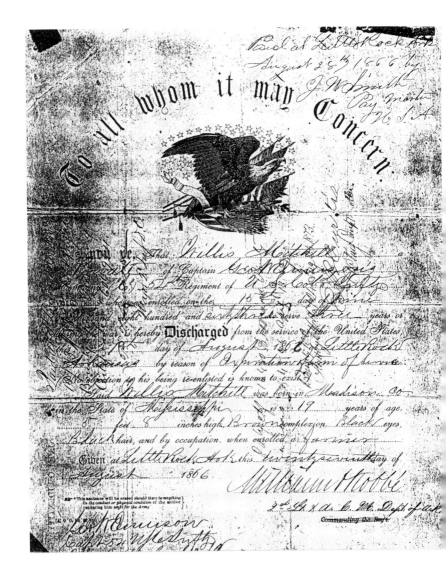

Uncle Mack and George Davis III

Mack Linole Houston was Medea Houston Mitchell's brother. Mack is buried in Quinette Cemetery.

Head Quarters District of St. Louis.

Office of Superintendent of Contrabands.

St. Louis, Mo., Aug 5th 1863.

Nancy Mitchell, a negro, aged 5 2 years, 5 ft 4 in ⟨...⟩ height, brown color, whose last master was John Wiley of Desha County, Arkansas State, is hereby declared to be an emancipated Slave, and a free man, by virtue of the Proclamation of the President of the United States, made 1st January, 1863, under the provisions of the Act of Congress of 17th July 1862.

By Order of Brig. General Strong,

Henry C. Fillebrown

Capt. and Chief of Staff.

Witness:

F. W. Newell

Chaplain and Superintendent of Contrabands.

Freedom papers for Nancy Mitchell, mother of James Anderson Mitchell.

The
George Washington
Willis
Family

George Washington Willis

Contributed by Rosetta Willis, who was a Massey Granddaughter and the daughter of Richard H. Willis. She lived in Kirkwood and died on June 20, 2001. Rosetta gave this information to a family member in order to document their family history.

My grandfather (paternal) George Washington Willis was born in Versailles, Kentucky (year unknown). Their parents were slaves.

Grandpa Willis was a sergeant in the civil war. I Rosetta Willis Massey (granddaughter), have a photograph of him in a blue uniform with sergeant's stripes. He and his wife came to Kirkwood, Mo (year unknown) settled on Holmes Avenue between East Main Street (name later changed to Argonne after World War I) and Madison Avenues. This settlement was called "Kentucky Town."

Names of their children:

1. Lucy Willis married Frank Monroe
2. Millie Willis married Mr. Turner
3. Emma Willis married Arthur (Dink) Ming
4. Daniel Willis married Lillie
5. William Willis married Hattie Terry
6. Ella Willis married
   a. Eddie Cheatman (passed)
   b. Harry McGee (passed)
   c. Ben Benton (passed)
7. Richard Henry Willis married Minnie Terry
8. Mary Willis (ran away from home and never heard from her)
9. Alexander Willis (don't remember his marriage status. He lives in Bridgeton. He had a stroke, unable to talk.)

George Washington Willis died in 1915
and is buried in Quinette Cemetery.

Service Record
of George
Washington Willis.

Hourglass Tree of George Washington Willis

Mildred E. Willis
Edward O. Willis
Mary T. Willis
Richard H. Jr.
George W. Willis
Rosetta V. Willis
Florence Willis
Elnora Willis

Alexander Willis
Tillie
Daniel Willis
Mamie A. Terry
Richard H. Willis 1883 - 1926
Hattie Terry 1873 -
William H. Willis 1879 -
Mary Willis
Ed Turner
Millie Willis

George W. Willis - 1915

Washington
Willis

Susan Banks

Aurther Dink Ming
Emma Willis
Eddie Cheatman
Ella Willis
Florence Smith
Susan Cheatman
Earl Monroe
Admathy
Fannie Monroe
Will Menser
Cussie Monroe
Gooden
Mamie Monroe
Lucy Willis
Frank Monroe

Robena Ming
Ralph Cheatman
William Admathy
Wanda Mae Menser
Babrbara Menser
Mildred Gooden

45

A Historical Sketch

of the

AME Church

and

Olive Chapel

AME Church

A Historical Sketch of the AME Church
and
Olive Chapel AME Church

The African Methodist Episcopal Church was started in 1787 in Philadelphia, Pennsylvania, by a group of disinherited Americans whose forefathers came from Africa. The leader of this group was a 27 year old "African," Richard Allen. The AME Church originated as a protest against the inhumane treatments which the helpless people of African descent were forced to accept from the white people belonging to the St. George Methodist Episcopal Church in Philadelphia. It expanded first on the eastern coast of the United States, thence westward and by 1841, William Paul Quinn, who became the 4th AME Bishop, had established the St. Paul AME Church in St. Louis, Missouri as the 1st AME church west of the Mississippi. Undoubtedly, other congregations were founded between 1841 and 1853, but Olive Chapel is the 2nd oldest AME Church west of the Mississippi. In 1853, Rev. Jordan Winston organized "The Olive Chapel of the African Methodist Episcopal Church" in Kirkwood.

Records of the early years of the Olive Chapel are fragmentary, but in Scharf's history of St. Louis City and County Published in 1883, reported that the little church was served by a circuit as the AME churches in Carondelet and Labadle. It is known that in 1864, the Rev. J. W. Early served the church and in 1865, the Rev. J. C. Embury conducted services.

Because of the lack of records, there is very little known about the history of Olive Chapel from 1865 until the Early 1920s.

In 1920, the church was fortunate to have the leadership of one Reverend M. S. Smith, a masterful pulpiteer, who carried on in the best tradition of African Methodism by fighting continuously for the civil rights of the Negro. He united with fellow ministers of Kirkwood to lead a fight for better educational opportunities for the Negro population in the Kirkwood community.

Like all endeavors, the churches has had its high and low periods in its march to the present day. For more than sixty years, all social life in the Negro community centered around the church and its literary society drew large numbers of people--both regular church-goers and non-church groups.

Many fine efforts that have benefited all of the people of Kirkwood had their beginning at Olive Chapel. The Kirkwood Civic Club, one of the most influential civic groups in St. Louis County, was spawned in Olive Chapel. The prize winning Booker Washington Playground Association was also started in Olive Chapel and piloted to great heights of success by Mr. and Mrs. George C. Davis, Jr. The Property Owners Protective Association also had its beginning in this historic church.

Olive Chapel has also produced several fine religious, professional, and civic and community leaders. Among them: Mrs. Myrtle McKinney Moffett, a St. Louis educator; Mrs. Daisy May Watson, a local and conference religious leader; Mrs. Pearl Bunch, a great spirit in missions and for whom along with Mrs. Watson, the local church Missionary Society was named: The Daisy-Pearl Missionary Society; Mr. George C. Davis Jr. and Mrs. Davis, know civic leaders, Mr. William Slaten, presently serving as President of the Federation of Block Units--Urban League;

Mrs. Patricia McKissack and her husband, Frederick, nationally known writers of children's books and winners of prestigious awards. Also, many exceptional contributions to the church, many of them sacrificial.

The Olive Chapel of the AME Church purchased property in 1923 at the corner of Monroe and Harrison Avenues. The congregation had been worshipping in a small stone building at 330 West Washington Avenue but had outgrown it. The West Washington address was also the site of Kirkwood's first public education classes for black students in 1867. The members of Olive Chapel came not only from the City of Kirkwood, but also from Meacham Park, Clayton, St. Louis and Oakland, so their new church gave them much needed space for expanded religious activities. Since that time, still at the corner of Monroe and Harrison, the church has continued to welcome people from far and near through its doors. The Olive Chapel building itself has been officially designated a Kirkwood Historic Landmark since 1981 and it is the 2nd oldest existent church in all of Kirkwood.

Our Pastors

1.	The Rev. Jordan Winston, Founder	1853
2.	The Rev. J. W. Early	1864
3.	The Rev. J. C. Embury	1865

Received Quinette Cemetery during his administration.

4.	The Rev. Moses Dickson	1868
5.	The Rev. James Madison	1870
6.	The Rev. I. N. Triplet	1872
7.	The Rev. W. A. Davis	1874
8.	The Rev. W. H. Saxton	1875
9.	The Rev. D. W. Oaks	1879
10.	The Rev. Hubbard Casper	1881
11.	The Rev. N. S. Parks	1882
12.	The Rev. N. H. Casper	1885
13.	The Rev. P. Thurman	
14.	The Rev. T. J. Townsend Stevenson	
15.	The Rev. R. L. Phillips	1906-1907
16.	The Rev. M. S. Smith	1921-1924

Congregation relocated from 330 W Washington to Harrison Ave during his administration.

17.	The Rev. R. L. Phillips	1927-1930
18.	The Rev. E. E. Tredwell	
19.	The Rev. William Burnett	
20.	The Rev. G. E. Horsey, M. D.	
21.	The Rev. B. Herron	
22.	The Rev. W. H. Lacey	
23.	The Rev. J. H. Matlock	1945-1949

Church mortgage was liquidated during his administration.

24.	The Rev. E. W. Hall	1949-1954
25.	The Rev. L. S. Goosby	1954-1956
26.	The Rev. E. G. Davis	1956-1958
27.	The Rev. R. L. Blackman	1958-1964
28.	The Rev. E. L. Strickland	1964-1966
29.	The Rev. E. W. Bevers	1966-1969
30.	The Rev. L. P. Parker	1969-1970
31.	The Rev. Wallace Ward	1970-1973
32.	The Rev. O. R. Booker	1973-1974
33.	The Rev. Milton Green	1975-1977
34.	The Rev. Jonathan Rhone	1977-1983
35.	The Rev. Ben Johnson	1983-1989
36.	The Rev. Charles Farris	1989-1992
37.	The Rev. Alvin Smith	1992-1994
38.	The Rev. Eugene Wright	1994-1997
39.	The Rev. Brenda J. Hayes	1998-2002
40.	The Rev. January F. Kiefer	2002-present

Conference year begins in October of each year. That's why pastors have overlapping years of service.

Kirkwood, Missouri

August 21, 1939

To Whom It May Concern:

As chairman of the committee for cleaning up Quinette Cemetery, I hereby make known the names of the following donors:

Mrs. Lizzie Walder	$1.00
Mrs. Joseph Harris	1.00
Mr. Sandford Ming	1.00
Mr. Ed Crittenden	1.00
Mr. Arthur Jones	1.00
Miss Martha Dunn	2.00
Miss Millie Dunn	2.00
Mr. George Davis Jr.	1.00
Mr. Walter Johnson	.50
Mr. Samuel Tyler	1.00
Mrs. Mamie Collins	1.00
Mr. George Davis Sr.	3.00
Mr. Harry Mitchell	1.00
Mr. J. P. Saunders	.50
Kirkwood Civic Club	1.00
Mr. George Broods Sr.	.50
Miss Myrtle McKinney	1.00
Mrs. Addie Ransome	.50
Mr. Arthur Whitson	.50
Mr. John Bouyer	2.00
Total----	22.50

This amount was paid to Charles Johnson for labor. With your continued assistance, we hope to keep this place in presentable order and I ask each of you to go out to the cemetery since the work is now completed.

George Davis Sr.

150 E. Monroe

Kirkwood, Missouri

United States Colored Troops and the Soldiers Buried in Quinette Cemetery

Colored Troops during the Civil War

When the Civil war began the concept of African-American inferiority was widely accepted. The Government at that time chose to maintain slavery through the Constitution which was adopted in 1845. Simply stated: "All persons of color who were slaves for life previous to their emigration to Texas, and who are now in bondage, shall remain in the state of servitude." Many blacks who had already been set free petitioned the government to maintain their freedom and property, most petitions were honored.

America was a planter society during the 1836 – 1845 decade and was still dependent on slave labor to do the work on the many plantations especially in the south. Slaves and free blacks existed side by side and because dual standards applied to these groups there was discontent among the slaves who were envious of the limited freedom of the free blacks. Relationships between the whites and blacks became increasingly strained and by the 1850's The North's anti-slavery attitude began to divide the country. In 1861 the Anti-slavery issue became part of the Civil War.

Blacks in the North were used in separate Union troops and blacks in the South were used to grow food and fiber for the Confederate Army and to care for the families of the plantation owners. Many slaves lost their lives trying to protect these families when Union troops overran Confederate lines.

The Union Army had suffered a series of defeats in 1861 and 1862, and the white enlisted decreased, Congress pressured President Lincoln to use African-Americans as soldier. Congress passed the Confiscation Act on August 6, 1861 which authorized the President to enlist African-Americans in the Army. President Lincoln still refused. Finally in October 1861, Secretary of War, Edwin Stanton authorized General Thomas W. Sherman to use all loyal persons offering their services for the defense of the Union.

Free blacks as well as slaves enlisted in the Union Army. They were in their own "Colored Troop" but had white officers in charge of their units. Many slaves ran away to become part of the Union Army. Plantation owners would mistreat or beat the mothers, wives and children of those who went to serve in the war. In an effort to stop this, plantation owners were paid by the government for their loss of slaves.

The efforts of the United States Colored Troops did not go unnoticed. On July 12, 1862, Congress established the Congressional Medal of Honor to recognize enlisted men of the armed services who distinguish themselves by gallantry in action. At least sixteen African- Americans received this commendation. Two examples of the USCT men in action who received a medal are Private James Gardner and Sergeant Major Christian A. Fleetwood. Pvt. Gardner of the 36th USCT rushed ahead of his brigade as they stormed the fort at New Market Heights. He shot and bayoneted a rebel officer who was rallying his forces. At Chaffin's Farm, Sgt-Mjr Fleetwood of the 4th USCT grabbed the union flag after two color guards had been shot. With no officers present, Fleetwood rallied a group of reserves to attack the fort during the final successful battle of the engagement.

There are several "Veterans of the Civil War" that are buried in Quinette Cemetery. Those known to be buried there are Washington Green, Willis Mitchell, James A. Mitchell, Henry Whitson and George Washington Willis. Arthur Mason was in the Army Reserves after the Civil War. The following is information from their Service Records and/or documents that family members shared.

65th REGIMENT INFANTRY.

Organized March 11, 1864, from 2nd Missouri Colored Infantry. Attached to Dept. of Missouri to June, 1864. Provisional Brigade, District of Morganza, La., Dept. of the Gulf, to September, 1864. 2nd Brigade, 1st Division, United States Colored Troops, District of Morganza, Dept. of the Gulf, to February, 1865. 1st Brigade, 1st Division, United States Colored Troops, District of Morganza, La., Dept. of the Gulf, to May, 1865. Northern District of Louisiana and Dept. of the Gulf to January, 1867.

SERVICE.—Garrison duty at Morganza, La., till May, 1865. Ordered to Port Hudson, La. Garrison duty there and at Baton Rouge and in Northern District of Louisiana till January, 1867. Mustered out January 8, 1867.

Regiment lost during service 6 Officers and 749 Enlisted men by disease.

65 Reg't U. S. C. T. Inf. Co. F

Whitson Henry

Rank ... Sergt ... Age 3X

Captain ... Hubbard ... Com'd'g.

Enlisted ... Dec 30 ... 63
Where ... Washington

Mustered in ... Jan 6 ... 6X
Where ... Benton Bks

Remarks ... Discharged Aug 15
1865 Consolidation

Mustered out ... Aug 15 = 1865
Where ... Baton Rouge La

56

Willis Mitchell

Regiment Name: 54 U.S. Col'd Infantry
Side: Union
Company: C
Soldier's Rank_In: Pvt
Soldier's Rank_Out: Pvt

54th Regiment, United States Colored Infantry

Organized March 11, 1864, from 2nd Arkansas Infantry (African Descent). Attached to
2nd Brigade, Frontier Division, 7th Corps, Dept. of Arkansas, to February, 1865. 2nd
Brigade, 1st Division, 7th Corps, to August, 1865. Dept. of Arkansas to December, 1866.

SERVICE- Duty at Helena, Ark., till May 1864. Ordered to Fort Smith, Ark., and duty
there till January, 1865. Actions at Fort Gibson September 16, 1864. Cabin Creek
September 19. Cow Creek, Kansas, November 14 and 28. Ordered to Little Rock
January, 1865. Action on Arkansas River January 18. Duty at Little Rock and at various
points in Dept. of Arkansas till December, 1866. Mustered out August 8 to December
31, 1866.

Washington Green
Regiment Name: 7 Missouri Infantry
Side: Union
Company: A
Soldier's Rank_In: C. Cook
Soldier's Rank_Out: C. Cook

Union Missouri Colunteers

7th Regiment, Missouri Infantry

Organized at St. Louis, Mo., June, 1861. Attached to Boonville, Mo., to September, 1861. Fremomt's Army of the West to February, 1862. Lexington, Mo., Dept. of the Missouri, to July, 1862. Unattached, Pittsburg Landing, Tenn., Army of the Tennessee, to September, 1862. 4th Brigade, 1st Division, District of Jackson, Tenn., to November, 1862. 4th Brigade, 3rd Division, Left Wing 13th Army Corps (Old), Dept. of the Tennessee, to December 1862. 3rd Brigade, 3rd Division, 17th Army Corps, to April, 1864. Maltby's Brigade, District of Vicksburg, Miss., to June, 1864. 1st Brigade, District of Memphis, Tenn., 16th Army Corps, to August, 1864 (Veterans). 1st Brigade, 2nd Division, 19th Army Corps, Dept. of the Gulf, to December, 1864.

SERVICE.- Moved to Booneville, Mo., July 1-4, 1861, thence to Rolla August 30 and to Syracuse, Mo., October 5-10. Fremont's Campaign against Springfield October 21- November 2. Moved to Sedalia November 10-14, thence to Otterville December and duty there till February, 1862. Expedition to Blue Springs January 20- February 3, 1862 (Cos. "B", "F" and "H" detached from Regiment November 21, 1861, and ordered to Kansas City. Rejoined Regiment at Lexington, Mo., February, 1862.) Moved to Lexington, Mo., February 3-10, 1862, and duty there till May 9. Reconnoissance from Greenville February 23-24 (Co. "H"). Skirmish at Mingo Creek near St. Francisville, February 24 (Co. "H"). Moved to Pittsburg Landing, Tenn., May 9-14, and guard and fatigue duty there till August 15. Moved to Jackson, Tenn., August 15-29, and duty there till October. Medon Station, Mississippi Central Railroad, August 31. Chewalla and Big Hill October 5, Medon Station October 10. Moved to Corinth with McPherson and to Jackson Octiober 14. To Lagrange November 2. Grant's Central Mississippi Campaign November 2, 1862, to January 10, 1863. At Memphis, Tenn., January 17 – February 21. Moved to Lake Providence, La.., February 21, and duty there till April. Moved to Milliken's Bend, La., April 12. Passage of Vicksburg batteries April 22 (Detachment). Movement on Bruinsburg and turning Grand Gulf April 25-39. Battle of Port Gibson May 1. Bayou Pierrie May 2. Battles of Raymond May 12. Champion Hill May 16. Big Black River Bridge May 17. Siege of Vicksburg, Miss. May 18- July 4. Assaults on Vicksburg May 19 and 22. Surrender of Vicksburg July 4. Provost duty there till June, 1864. Stevenson's Expedition from Vicksburg to Monroe, La., August 20- September 2, 1863. Expedition toward Canton October 14-22. Bogue Chitto Creek October 17. Expedition from Vicksburg to Sunnyside Landing, Ark., January 10-16, 1864. Meridian Campaign February 3- March 2. Clinton February 5. Veterans on furlough March and May.

Henry Whitson

Regiment Name: 65 U.S. Col'd Infantry
Side: Union
Company: F
Soldier's Rank_In: Pvt
Soldier's Rank_Out: Sgt

65th Regiment, United States Colored Infantry

Organized March 11, 1864, from 2nd Missouri Colored Infantry. Attached to Dept. of Missouri to June, 1864. Provisional Brigade, District of Morganza, La., Dept. of the Gulf, to September, 1864. 2nd Brigade, 1st Division, United States Colored Troops, District of Morganza, Dept. of the Gulf, to February, 1865. 1st Brigade, 1st Division, United States Colored Troops, District of Morganza, La., Dept. of the Gulf, to May, 1865. Morthern District of Louisiana and Dept. of the Gulf to January, 1867.

SERVICE- Garrison duty at Morganza, La., till May 1865. Ordered to Port Hudson, La. Garrison duty there and at Baton Rouge and in Northern District of Louisiana till January, 1867. Mustered out January 8, 1867.

Regiment lost during service 6 Officers and 749 Enlisted men by disease.

65th Regiment Infantry
Organized March 11, 1864, from 2nd Missouri Colored Infantry. Attached to
Dept. of Missouri to June, 1864. Provisional Brigade, District of Morganza, La., Dept. of
the Gulf, to September, 1864. 2nd Brigade, 1st Division, United States Colored Troops,
District of Morganza, Dept. of the Gulf, to February, 1865. 1st Brigade, 1st Division,
United States Colored Troops, District of Morganza, La., Dept. of the Gulf, to May,
1865. Northern District of Louisiana and Dept. of the Gulf to January, 1867.

SERVICE--Garrison duty at Morganza, La., till May, 1965. Ordered to Port
Hudson, La. Garrison duty there and at Baton Rouge and in Northern District of
Louisiana till January, 1867. Mustered out January 8, 1867.

Regiment lost during service 6 Officers and 749 Enlisted men by disease.

297: Officer in a Missouri Black Regiment to
the Superintendent of the Organization of
Missouri Black Troops

Benton Barracks, Mo. February 6, 1864.

Sir-- I have just received information-by Sergt Whitson of my Company just from St.
Clare--that the wives of Simon Williamson & Richard Beasley has again been whiped by
their Master most unmercyfully. Their Master is one John Crowder and lives about three
miles this side of the village of St. Clare in Franklin County. He refuses to let them go to
Post Office to get their letters, and if anyone comes to them and brings them letters and
reads them to them he is shure to whip then for it if he knows is. Williamson & Beasley
are members of my company and are good Soldiers. If any thing could be done to relieve
their families it would afford me a good deel satisfaction and relieve them from a good
deel of anxiety. Very respectfully your Ob't Serv't,
A. J. Hubbard

Arthur Mason
Pvt. 1st Class 442 Res

Arthur Mason was born on March 1, 1881 in Tennessee, and died February 22, 1938 at the age of 56. He lived in Kirkwood at the time of his death. His parents were Bob Mason and Susanna Camron or Caumon of Tennessee. Arthur Mason was never married and had no children.

Arthur was inducted into the military on August 10, 1918 and served in the 159 DEP Brig to November 12, 1918 and then Company B 442 Reserve Labor BN to March 19, 1919. He was honorably Discharged as a PVT 1-19.

His burial was March 1, 1938 in Quinette Cemetery. He did not receive a military funeral; however, a family member or friend purchased a military headstone that was placed on his grave sight. The military headstone still exists today in Quinette Cemetery, it is one of the few grave markers left untouched by vandals and time. It is located about 300 feet into the cemetery and to the right. It is about six feet from a small house currently being used as a business named the Miller Group.

MISSISTOURI STATE BOARD OF HEALTH
BUREAU OF VITAL STATISTICS
CERTIFICATE OF DEATH

File No. **8096**

Registration District No. **96**

Primary Registration District No.

Registered No. **379**

No. Clayton Ave. (Emma A. Hope Jr.) Ward.

PERSONAL AND STATISTICAL PARTICULARS

1. PLACE OF DEATH

   County St. Louis

   Township Clayton

   City Clayton

2. FULL NAME Arthur Mason

   (a) Residence. No. 401 So. Hanley St. Ward.

   (Usual place of abode) (If nonresident, give city or town and State)

   Length of residence in city or town where death occurred 7 yrs. mos. da. How long in U.S., if of foreign birth? yrs. mos. da.

3. SEX	4. COLOR OR RACE	5. SINGLE, MARRIED, WIDOWED OR DIVORCED
Male	Col	Single

5a. IF MARRIED, WIDOWED, OR DIVORCED HUSBAND OF, OR WIFE OF

6. DATE OF BIRTH (MONTH, DAY, AND YEAR) March 1-1881

7. AGE		
YEARS	MONTHS	DAYS	If LESS than 1 day, hrs. or min.
56	11	26	

8. Trade, profession, or particular kind of work done, as spinner, sawyer, bookkeeper, etc. Janitor

9. Industry or business in which work was done, as silk mill, saw mill, bank, etc.

10. Date deceased last worked at this occupation (month and year)

11. Total time (years) spent in this occupation 1

12. BIRTHPLACE (CITY OR TOWN) STATE OR COUNTRY) West Virginia

13. NAME

14. BIRTHPLACE (CITY OR TOWN, STATE OR COUNTRY) Susanna Cannon

15. MAIDEN NAME Susanna Cannon

16. BIRTHPLACE (CITY OR TOWN) STATE OR COUNTRY)

17. INFORMANT Mrs. Hilmes

    ADDRESS St. Louis

18. BURIAL, CREMATION, OR REMOVAL

    PLACE Cremation DATE Mch

19. UNDERTAKER Hilmes

    ADDRESS

20. FILED 3-1-1938 F. R. Ruppolt Registrar.

MEDICAL CERTIFICATE OF DEATH

21. DATE OF DEATH (MONTH, DAY, AND YEAR) **Feb. 26 1938**

22. I HEREBY CERTIFY, That I attended deceased from ____ 19 , to ____ 19 .

    I last saw h alive on ____ 19 . Death is said to have occurred on the date stated above, at **5:45 AM**

    The principal cause of death and related causes of importance were as follows:

    Date of onset

    Syphilis of Heart

    Other contributory causes of importance:

    Name of operation ____ Date of ____

    What test confirmed diagnosis? Autopsy Was there an autopsy **Yes**

23. If death was due to external causes (violence), fill in also the following:

    Accident, suicide, or homicide? ____ Date of injury ____ 19

    Where did injury occur? ____

    (Specify city or town, county, and State)

    Specify whether injury occurred in industry, in home, or in public place.

    Manner of injury ____

    Nature of injury ____

24. Was disease or injury in any way related to occupation of deceased **No**

    If so, specify

    (Signed) John E. Grindel M.D.

    (Address) Coroner of St. Louis County

62

Funeral Practices

of the

late 1800's

and

early 1900's

Funeral Practices of the late 1800's & early 1900's

Contributed By John D. Avery

During the time period that Quinette Cemetery was most used, roughly the last quarter of the 1800's and the first quarter of the 1900's, there was not a great deal of change in funeral practices in West St. Louis County, Missouri. However, Quinette Cemetery being an African American cemetery there would possibly be some ethnic differences in funeral practices. This discussion will center on some of the common funeral practices of the time.

This **fourth quarter – first quarter** period, as I will refer to it, was a time when death still entered the family circle in a very intimate and far too often way. It was usual for the end of the life spectrum, illness and death, to be a part of the family experience, just as it was for the beginning of the life spectrum, birth. Ones' life and death often came full circle within the family home. This was true even more so for those with limited financial means. There were few hospitals and only the financially able or more unusual medical cases might be taken there for treatment. Because of medical practice and scientific knowledge being yet in its infancy, there were many deaths even in the hospital.

With West St. Louis County still being largely populated by people living an agrarian or country lifestyle, most extended families lived within close proximately. Therefore, when there was a death, the extended family would come together and support each other in whatever way was needed at the time. This might be the preparing of meals for the immediate family, tending to the fields and crops, taking care of the younger children or preparing the home for the wake and funeral. It was around World War I, that family members began moving away.

They might be looking for better jobs or excitement or just seeing the world. Travel became more accessible and affordable.

During the fourth quarter and into the early first quarter the immediate family would probably do all but the final "laying out". In the poorer families even th would be done by members of the family. The body would be washed and dressed in his or her finest garments. The parlor or main room of the house might b prepared by moving furniture out of the way to make way for the burial coffin c casket and room for the visitors to make their way to view the body. Other funer customs might also be observed. Black crepe or a black wreath might be placed c the front door signifying to those passing by that there had been a death in th home. In some families older customs still survived, such as draping mirrors ar portraits in the home.

If the undertaker or funeral director (a yet seldom used title) was available provide the burial coffin or casket, and the family could afford one, it would l brought to the home. The body would then be placed in it and the burial coffin casket would be placed in the parlor on casket stands, barrels or even two chair The undertaker might also bring chairs and other needed funeral paraphernalia in the home at the request of the family. The extent of the involvement of t undertaker depended in large part on the financial ability of the family. The hon and family were now ready for visitors. In the event that the family did not ha money enough to secure the services of the undertaker, it would be common for family member or friend to make the coffin and provide it as a gift to t immediate family.

The *wake* or visitation was a time for the friends and neighbors to come to the home and pay their respects to the family on the death of the loved one. It was a common practice to take food to the home immediately following the death or as soon as news of the death was received.. Depending on two major factors, the time of year, and the distance between family members, the wake could be from one to three days in length. If the death occurred when the weather was hot and humid, the wake would last but be a short period of time, maybe only a day. In the poorer white families and most all of the ethnic families, embalming to preserve the body was not at all a common practice. If the death occurred in cooler weather the decaying of the body would not be as rapid, so the body could be held a longer period of time before burial.

During the fourth quarter –first quarter period in our history there were still only three types of funeral in common practice. The funeral home as we know it today, was not yet in common use. Having the funeral in the home was the usual practice. In that the wake had taken place in the home, it was easy for the clergy person simply to come to the home, have the service in the parlor and then take the casket to the cemetery. For those families whose faith, church and tradition held a central place in their lives, it would have been customary to transport the casket to the church for the funeral service or Mass. The burial coffin or casket would have been transported by a horse drawn hearse, if money was available, or by a wagon of some sort. The undertaker would have provided the hearse. If a wagon was used, it might have belonged to a family member or friend. It was also a common practice to have a simple grave side service at the cemetery. There would not be a wake or viewing. The burial casket of coffin would have been taken directly to the cemetery where a few words might be said over the body after which the burial container would be lowered into the grave.

The customs and services were similar for both black and white families of the lat 1800's and the early 1900's. There was and is a greater difference in the grieving customs and traditions. However, this is a topic for another time an place.

The selection of burial coffins and caskets was limited during this time perio Styles might vary some, but typically they were very similar. Plate #1 is a litho a common coffin shaped wooden burial container. This was still used into th early 1900's by poorer folk.

PLATE #1

The familiar coffin shaped burial container

Litho courtesy of Criswell Casket Company, St. Louis, Missouri

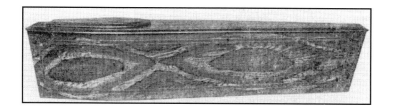

PLATE #2

Coffin shaped burial container with glass viewing panel and wooden cover

Print courtesy of he Museum of Funeral Custom, 1440 Monument Ave., Springfield, Illinois,

The third Plate, shows the more favored cloth covered wood casket. This type of burial casket became widely used is the early years of the 1900's. It was still inexpensive, though slightly more in cost than the wooden coffins. It did have much nicer eye appeal however.

Plate #3

Octagon cloth covered wood casket

Print courtesy of the Museum of Funeral Custom, 1440 Monument Ave., Springfield, Illinois

The metal burial container or casket that is familiar today did not gain in popularit until into the 1920's. It was considerably more expensive than any of the buria containers discussed here and was undoubtedly not used in Quinette Cemetery i the earlier years.

As you can see, the early years of Quinette Cemetery were simple ones. This wa true in burial practices in general. Yes, family financial circumstances did play part in these practices, as they have throughout history, but for the most part li and death was still very simple in rural America.

1860's Horse Drawn Hearse owned and retored by John D. Avery of Manchester Missouri.

Bopp Chapel
Over 100 Years
of Service

Over 100 Years of Service - Bopp Chapel

We have come a long way in the area of personal funeral service. Today there are gift shops located in funeral homes. There are on-line obituaries that include photographs, personal history and a place for memorials, all of which have world-wide access. In the state of Colorado there is a "Drive-Thru" funeral home for those who do not want to get out of their cars or only have a few minutes to pay their respects.

The families of the loved ones buried in Quinette did not have all these things available then. Most of them did not have a big funeral, nor did they have flowers or a guest book for people to sign and of those who could afford a gravestone about 90 percent of the gravestones in Quinette Cemetery are now gone. Some gravestones have deteriorated over the years and others have been vandalized or stolen which is a felony under the law.

In the state of Missouri there are many laws in place which make it illegal to remove, damage, destroy or otherwise vandalize a cemetery. The Cemetery Laws of the State of Missouri can be found in their entirety in the appendix. Below are some of those laws which may be especially helpful in understanding the governing of cemeteries. A few of those laws are as follows:

1. Any person, corporation, partnership, proprietorship, or organization who knowingly disturbs, destroys, vandalizes, or damages a marked or unmarked human burial site commits a class D felony.   *Mo. Statute 194.410*

2. No road shall be constructed in any cemetery over a burial lot in which dead human remains are buried.   *Mo. Statute 214.041*

3. Every person who shall knowingly destroy, mutilate, disfigure, deface, injure, or remove any tomb, monument, or gravestone, or other structure placed in any abandoned family cemetery or private burying ground, or any fence, railing, or other work for protection of ornamentation of any such cemetery or place of burial of any human being, or tomb, monument, or memorial, or any other structure aforesaid, or of any lot within such cemetery is guilty of a class A misdemeanor.   *Mo. Statues 214.131*

4. Whenever the attorney general determines the existence of an abandoned cemetery in this state, the attorney general shall immediately proceed to dissolve the cemetery corporation owning the same. Upon the dissolution of such corporation, title to all property owned by the cemetery corporation shall vest in the municipality or county in which the cemetery is located.   *Mo. Statues 214.205-2*

5. ... every municipality or county in which any abandoned cemetery is located may acquire through its power of eminent domain such cemetery, together with all endowed care funds, maintenance equipment, books and records. Upon so acquiring the cemetery and related property, the acquiring municipality or county shall operate and maintain the cemetery as a public cemetery.   *Mo. Statues 214.205-3*

Over 100 Years of Service - Bopp Chapel

The laws are in place to assure families that the final resting place of their deceased loved one will not be disturbed or desecrated in any way. Prior to the final resting place these families rely on funeral directors and other staff at funeral homes to help them with the final arrangements. The State of Missouri also established The Missouri Board of Embalmers and Funeral Directors in 1895 to govern the practices of funeral homes. Once such funeral home is Bopp Chapel.

Bopp Chapel has been a family owned funeral home for over 100 years. Founder and owner Louis Henry Bopp established Bopp Chapel in Kirkwood in March of 1902. Louis had a livery service on West Jefferson in Kirkwood. It was determined that some type of funeral service was needed and Bopp Chapel was created. In 1918, Bopp Chapel moved to West Argonne. In 1931 a second location was opened in Clayton and in 1961 both locations were consolidated into one location on Manchester Road in Kirkwood where they continue to operate today.

In an interview with Christine A. Bopp, she stated that in the "good old days" (early 1900's} if you had enough money, you could buy an "ice coffin". This was a coffin which had boards on the sides, sort of like a trough, where they would place ice, to keep the body cold.

In an interview Richard Mueller, Jr., one of the funeral directors for Bopp Chapel, had with some youngsters from Robinson School, in 1999, he stated that Bopp Chapel held approximately 600 funerals and sold about 500 caskets per year. An average of two people were cremated there each week and one of their Hearses would leave for a funeral about twice a day.

Bopp Chapel has been in the business of service the community in their time of need for over 100 years and remains family owned and operated. Mr. Louis Bopp and his family cared very much about the quality of service they offered to the community, as well as caring very much for and about the people they served. Bopp Chapel has a history of going out of their way to assist and be of service to the families and friends of the loved ones who have passed on. Some of those extra touches include things like picking someone up to attend the funeral service, getting doughnuts for those who request them, and assisting with balloons or other items to be on display for the visitation or funeral service. That strong tradition of outstanding quality service and caring started by Louis Bopp continues to this day.

The Merchant's Day Parade passes by Bopp Livery and Undertaker on July 4, 1907.

Louis H. Bopp readies his entry in the Merchant's Day Parade on July 4, 1907.

Louis H. Bopp's newest Horse drawn Hearse in the early 1900's.

Quinette Cemetery Today

Quinette Cemetery is the oldest, ethnic cemetery in St., Louis County. It serves as a final resting place to many African Americans who were poor or enslaved during their lifetime. In 1961, developers began encroaching on Quinette Cemetery when commercial buildings were built on the east side of the cemetery. Trees were cut down and head stones were knocked over and moved. The cemetery soon looked like a trash dump. The City of Kirkwood sent letters and made many attempts to contact Olive Chapel AME Church, the owners of the cemetery. The cemetery was not being maintained properly and weeds were overtaking the property.

In 1978, The Kirkwood City Council passed an ordinance for the termination of the cemetery and the removal and eventually sold the Quinette Cemetery property to Edward Weinhardt, who owned and operated the Green Parrot Restaurant and other land adjacent to the cemetery. During his ownership, the cemetery continued its state of decline. Head stones were overturned and trash was ever present; a tragic state of affairs for Quinette, one of only five known African-American slave burial grounds in the state of Missouri.

In 2002, a developer, Miracle Design, had purchased the property from Weinhardt and was given approval by the Kirkwood City Council, to build 10 two-family attached residences on the site. In addition, the Green Parrot Restaurant would be converted back into a single-family residence. The development, known as "The Sommet," includes a unique stormwater management plan that features 29-inch rain gardens scattered throughout the site to absorb water runoff. The Metropolitan Sewer District, as well as the Department of Natural Resources, said, "It (the stormwater plan) is an approach that the recognizes the importance of designing buildings that work in harmony with nature."

As part of the development agreement, Miracle Design agreed to deed the cemetery over to the City of Kirkwood and contribute $50,000 to establish a fund for the future care and maintenance of the cemetery. A wrought-iron fence will be constructed to help shield the cemetery.

Kirkwood Mayor Mike Swoboda hopes the city will take possession of Quinette Cemetery sometime in 2003, the year Kirkwood celebrates its 150th anniversary, at which time a dedication ceremony will take place. A task force will also be appointed to oversee the historical values of the cemetery and its importance to the community.

Photographs of Quinette today taken in 2002 by Keith Rawlings.

A list of those
known to be buried
in Quinette Cemetery

Quinette Cemetery, established 1866, 12200 Old Big Bend at Ballas, Kirkwood, MO 63122

Name		Born	Died	Age
("D")				
Baker, Julia	wife of Isaac Baker	1855	July 12, 1883	28 years
Bell, Birdie		1873	1874	1 year
Bell, Lillie		1873	1874	7 months
Bouyer, Charlie	twin of John Bouyer			
Bouyer, Cloe				
Bouyer, John	twin of Charlie Bouyer			
Bouyer, Laura				
Bouyer, Linnie				
Bouyer, Sallie				
Bouyer, Sam				
Bouyer, Sophie	husband & father	1828	1911	83 years
Bowles, James	wife & mother			
Bowles, Mary		1816	June 13, 1885	71 years
Boyd, Gideon		August 19, 1889	January 27, 1901	12 years
Boyd, Milton			May 10, 1901	
Carter, Mary		1800	1900	100 years
Dunn, George Andrew				
Gray, George W			1903	
Green, Mathilda				
Green, Washington	7th Inf. Co. A Col'd Cook			
Grey, Kirkey				
Houston, Linole Mack				
J. B.				
J. R.				
Johnson, John				
Johnson, Perline				
Jones, Emma				
Jones, James (Jimmy)				
Martin, Alcy		1832	1912	80 years
Martin, John		1836		
Martin, Rev. W. M.				

87

Quinette Cemetery, established 1866, 12200 Old Big Bend at Ballas, Kirkwood, MO 63122

Name	Born	Died	Age
Mason, Arthur — Pvt. 1st Class 442 Res.		February 26, 1938	
Mitchell, James Anderson — 33rd Degree Mason	1856	1885	29 years
Mitchell, Meda Cornelia Houston — Co. C 54th Regiment U.S. Col'd Infty?			
Mitchell, Willis	1847		
Morris, Napoleon B.	May 10, 1832	August 23, 1887	55 years
Porter, John			
Rice, Abraham			
Rice, Easter			
Rice, Lucind	1836		
Rice, Richard	1878	1878	
Rice, Robert	1865	1873	
Spears, "Baby" (Child of William Walter & Josephene Spears)			
Spears, Hannah			
Spears, Sandy Manassa JR	1857	May 20, 1916	41 years
Spears, Walter Lambert			
St. James, Harriet			
Steele, Willie	1858	1873	
Taylor, Henry			
Thompson, Abraham			
Turner, John			
Whitson, Henry — 65th U.S. CT Inf. Co. F	1831	1878	47 years
Willis, George Wahington — 41st Inf. Co. E		1914 or 1915	
Woodbridge, Joseph			
Wooldrige, Joseph	1881		

88

Tombstone Rubbings

One of the best ways to read the information on old tombstones is to make a rubbing of it. In order to get a clear rubbing that is easy to read you will need the following items:

Large newsprint paper
Black charcoal sticks– flat edge
Turkey baster
Disposable rubber gloves
Masking tape
Handi-wipes

To get started, use the Turkey Baster to blow the dirt out of the etched lettering on the tombstone. Next, tape the newsprint paper to the tombstone covering the letters that you wish to do the rubbing of. Put on the rubber gloves and take a black charcoal stick and using the flat edge gently move it up and down the paper starting at one side of the paper and working across to the other side until you have rubbed the entire etched print. Do not press too hard on the paper as tearing can occur. Use the handi-wipes to clean your hands, etc. When you are finished you will have a clear print of the information that is on the tombstone.

Keith Rawlings making a rubbing of a tombstone in Quinette Cemetery.
The tombstone is of Isaac Baker who died July 12, 1883 at the age of 28.

BIRDY BELL
1874 June ? Age 1 Year

LILLIE BELL
1874 Age 7 Months

NAPOLEON B. MORRIS
May 10, 1832 – Aug. 23, 1887

Rubbings by Harlow P. Donovan

90

Closing

When I set out to write this book there was very little information about Quinette Cemetery and the people buried within its boundries. The Kirkwood Historical Society did not have any information available. We started with the names that could be read on the existing tombstones and photos of tombstones that existed in 1964-65. A list of names was compiled and the research began. Through contact with remaining family members of those known to be buried there we were able to add to the list of names. The list remains incomplete as there are others buried there in unmarked graves.

The last known burial at Quinette was in 1973 by a minister and his wife who lived next to the cemetery. No one knows how old the baby was or whether it was a boy or girl since the minister and his wife are now deceased.

Through this book I hope to generate interest in the preservation of Quinette Cemetery. It is a part of history and there are many stories yet to be told. Hopefully, the City of Kirkwood will honor those buried there with new headstones as they are permanent residents of Kirkwood.

Directory
Of The
City of Kirkwood

~1910 ~
CONTAINING

Names and locations of residences of all persons of eighteen years of age or over.

Names and location of all streets.

Location of all churches, with pastors names and time of all meetings.

Names of city officials.

Location of public places.

Time and place of meeting of all lodges.

Street car time tables and route of tracks.

Railroad time table.

Advertisements of the progressive business men of Kirkwood and elsewhere.

Kirkwood Officials and Public Places

Mayor.. J. H. Knierim
City Attorney.. E. R. Chappell
City Clerk.. A. L. Ossenfort
City Collector... R. W. Crutsinger
City Treasurer... T. D. Kimball
Police Judge..H. S. Jacobi
City Marshal..W. L. Kinyon
Street Commissioner..William Bell

BOARD OF ALDERMEN

First Ward -- H. G. Wyer and J. R. French.
Second Ward -- F. Rott and J. C. Page.
Third Ward -- Thos. W. Corley and J. W. Weber.
Fourth Ward -- J. C. Berthold and John Milliken.
The regular sessions of the Board are held on the first Monday in each month in the boardroom, Madison ave., between Webster and Clay avenues.

FIRE DEPARTMENT

Chief -- D. C. Berg. First assistant Chief -- August Bopp. Second Assistant Chief -- Brown. Secretary -- Wm. Donworth. Assistant Secretary -- Lon Kinyon. Treasurer Kelly. Hook and Ladder Captain -- Chas. Lenz. Salvage Captain -- Alex. Doerr. Hose C -- Ed Durand, George Billings. Executive Committee -- Wm. Knierim, Geo. F. Kerth, L Bopp, Peter Prough, Chas. Lenz.

PUBLIC PLACES

Post Office -- Webster and Madison avenues.
City Clerkís Office, 111 W. Madison avenue.
City Collectorís Office, Webster and Madison avenues.
Electric Light Plant, Taylor and Monroe avenues.
Fire Department, Jefferson between Webster and Clay avenues.
High School, Grammar School, Kindergarten, on Adams, Clay, and Jefferson.
Choral Hall, West Bodley avenue.
St. Peterís Hall, Main street and Clay avenue.
W. C. T. U. Hall, S. E. Cor. Clay and Adams avenues.

Church Directory

ST. PETERíS CATHOLIC CHURCH -- Main St. between Clay and Harrison.
Rev. B. G. Stemker, Pastor. Res. 213 W. Main St.
First mass, 8 oíclock Sunday morning. High mass and benediction at 10:30.
Arch confraternity of the Holy Rosary on 1st Sunday of each month at 3 p. m.

BAPTIST CHURCH -- Southwest corner Webster and Washington avenues.
Rev. Burtt N. Timbie, Pastor. Res. 120 E. Monroe Ave.
Preaching every Sunday morning at 10:45 and evening at 7:30.
Sunday School, 9:30 a. m.   B. Y. P. U. at 7 p. m.
Prayer meeting Wednesday evening at 8.

GRACE CHURCH -- Southeast corner Main street and Taylor avenue.
Rev. L. F. Potter, Rector. Res. 143 E. Adams Avenue.
Holy communion, 7:30, a. m.   Sunday school, 9:45 a. m.
Midday service, 11 a. m.   Evensong, 4:30 p. m.

METHODIST CHURCH -- Southwest corner Clay and Washington avenue.

METHODIST CHURCH -- Southwest corner Clay and Washington avenue.

L. R. Jenkins, Pastor. Res. 521 N. Clay Avenue.

Preaching at 10:45 a. m. and 8:00 p. m. Sunday.   Sunday school at 9:30 a. m.

Prayer meeting Wednesday at 8 p. m.   Epworth League, 6:45 p. m. Sunday.

PRESBYTERIAN CHURCH -- Southeast corner Webster and Adams avenues

Preaching at 10:45 a. m. and 8:00 p. m.   Sunday school, 9:30 a. m.

Christian Endeavor, 6:45 p. m.   Prayer meeting, Wednesday 8 p. m.

CONCORDIA GERMAN LUTHERAN CHURCH -- Taylor and Clinton Pl.

Rev. Theodore F. Walther, Pastor. Res. 136 E. Clinton Place

Preaching every Sunday at 10 a. m.

English preaching every first and third Sunday at 7:30 p. m.

FIRST CHURCH OF CHRIST, SCIENTIST -- N. W. corner Clay and Washington avenues.

H. C. Ochterbeck, First Reader, 340 E. Main

Lesson Sermon, Sunday 10:45 a. m.; Sunday School, 9:45 a. m. Testimonial Meeting, Wednesday at 8:15 p. m. Reading Room, N. E. corner of Jefferson and Webster, open week days, 2 to 5. p. m.

COLORED CHURCHES

A. M. E. CHURCH --Washington and Van Buren avenues.

Rev. P. Thurman, Pastor.

Sunday school 9:30 a. m.   Preaching 11 a. m. and 7:30 p. m.

SECOND BAPTIST CHURCH --Taylor and Monroe avenues.

Rev. Brown, Pastor.

Sunday school 9:30 a. m.   Preaching 11 a. m. and 7:30 p. m.

HARRISON AVENUE BAPTIST -- Harrison and Clinton.

Rev. Samuel Tyler, Pastor.

Sunday school 9:30 a. m.   Preaching 11 a. m. and 7:30 p. m.

FIRST BAPTIST CHURCH -- Railroad street and Clinton Place.

Rev. Robt Lucas, Pastor.

Preaching at 7:30 p. m.

LODGES

The following lodges and associations meet at Masonic Hall, southwest corner Webster and Adams avenues.

J. U. O. A. M. -- First and third Mondays.

A. F. & A. M. -- Second and fourth Mondays.

W. O. W. -- Second and fourth Tuesdays.

M. W. A. -- Second and fourth Wednesdays.

L. of H. -- First Tuesday.

R. A. -- Second Thursday.

K. O. T. M. -- First Friday.

CLUBS

Kirkwood Monday Evening Club. Stanley D. Pearce, President; Mrs. C. H.
    Mclean, Secretary.

The Kirkwood Piano Club. Miss Amy B. Chandler, President; Mrs. Howard
    Ewald, Secretary.

Mercantile Club. Frank E. Lautz, President; Harry Donovan, Secretary.

The Fortnightly Club of Kirkwood. Mrs. William Clegg Jr. President; Mrs.
    Franklin Kean, Corresponding Secretary.

Business Menís Credit Association - Third Tuesday in Mercantile Club rooms 207 N.
Webster avenue.

~ DIRECTORY OF ~
RESIDENTS OF KIRKWOOD

~A~

Abadie, E H, consulting engineer, 502 S Webster ave
Abadie, Mrs Annis B, 502 S Webster ave
Abbott, Mrs S S, 221 Way ave
Abehart, Anne, maid, 517 S Webster
Abrams, Geo G, 424 N Clay ave
Abrams, Mrs Harriet S, 424 N Clay ave
Adams, Chas F, 607 W Monroe ave
Adams, Mrs Leona, 607 W Monroe ave
Admath, Clara, colored, 421 S Harrison ave
Admath, Dennis, colored, 421 S Harrison ave
Ahner, Rev G E, florist, 750 N Woodlawn ave
Ahner, Mrs Elizabeth, 750 N Woodlawn ave
Ahner, Pual, carpenter, 750 N Woodlawn ave
Ahner, Johanna, 325 Dickson st.
Alberty, David, colored, 205 N Van Buren ave
Alberty, Mrs Mattie, colored, 205 N Van Buren ave
Albright, Mrs N O, boarding house, 135 E Washington ave
Albright, Orrick, clerck United Railways, 135 E Washington ave
Albright, W A, postmaster, 503 S Webster ave
Albright, Mrs Elizabeth, 503 S Webster ave
Albright, Miss Clara P, teacher, 503 S Webster ave
Albright, Miss Jessie C, 503 S Webster ave
Alexander, B C, laborer, 117 E Monroe ave
Alexander, Mrs M L, 117 E Monroe ave
Alexander, Mary, colored, cook, 326 E Main st
Alger, J F, with Hamilton Brown Shoe Co, 234 E Main st

Alger, Mrs M Lou, 234 E Main st
Alger, F W, office clerck Wabash R R, 234 E Main st
Allen, Harry, clk County Recorderíd office, 104 W Madison ave
Allcn, Mrs Barbara, 104 W Madison ave
Allen, Mrs N H, 219 S Taylor ave
Allen, Lizzie, colored, servant, Woodlawn Hotel
Allen, Emma, colored, servant, Woodlawn Hotel
Allen, Geneva, colored, servant, Woodlawn Hotel
Alter, G D, Baggageman Mo Pacific R R, 118 W Jefferson ave
Alter, Mrs J E, 118 W Jefferson ave
Alter, Robert, 118 W Jefferson ave
Alter, Edith, teacher, 118 W Jefferson ave
Alter, Bessie, 118 W Jefferson ave
Alter, Howard, Mo Pac shop, 206 W Main st
Alter, Howard, Mo Pac brakeman, 517 N Harrison ave
Alter, Mrs Howard, 517 N Harrison ave
Alter, W W, clerck Holekamp Lumber Co, 117 E Jefferson ave
Alter, Mrs E M, 117 E Jefferson ave
Alter, Alice, teacher, 117 E Jefferson ave
Ambler, A B, Travelers Ins Co, Gill ave
Ambler, Mrs C K, Gill ave
Ambler, T M, Backus Light Co, 215 N Taylor ave
Ambler, Mrs Carrie H, 215 N Taylor ave
Ambler, Willis H, 215 N Taylor ave
Andrews, Mrs H M, 350 S Clay ave
Andrews, John, colored, 409 S Harrison ave
Andrews, Mrs Catherine, colored, 409 S Harrison ave
Andrews, Lyda, colored maid, 522 S Clay ave
Andrews, W G, engineer Kirkwood Laundry, 571 S Clay ave
Andrews, Mrs Jennie, 571 S Clay ave
Anglin, J H, traveling salesman, 112 N Harrison ave
Anglin, Mrs M S, 112 N Harrison ave
Anth, Chas, 232 W Essex ave
Anth, Mrs Caroline, 232 W Essex ave
Anth, Wm, butcher, 431 W Essex ave
Anth, Mrs Margaret, 431 W Essex ave
Armentrout, Chas, Restaurant and Confectionary, Main and Clay avenues,
    Res 210 W Main st
Armentrout, Mrs M, 210 W Main st
Armentrout, Mrs Laura A, 206 W Main st
Armentrout, Louis, painter, 206 W Main st
Armentrout, T W, 200 W Main st
Armentrout, Mrs Rose, 200 W Main st
Armstrong, Georgia, maid, 505 N Taylor ave
Arthur, Anna, maid, 321 N Harrison ave
Asbridge, Ettie, maid, 521 N Clay ave
Ashley, George, mail carrier, 736 N Webster ave
Ashley, Edward F, carpenter, 736 N Webster ave
Ashley, Hood, carpenter, 736 N Webster ave

Ashley, Mrs Emma, 736 N Webster ave
Ashley, Susan, 736 N Webster ave
Atwell, Miss Eliza, 219 E Washington ave
Austin, Jas, R R Conítr, 472 N Webster ave
Austin, Mrs Laura, 472 N Webster ave
Ayres, Miss Evelyn, teacher, 230 E Main st

OUTSIDE CITY LIMITS

Anderson, Jennie H, Sappington road and Adams ave
Anthony, J W, Meacham Park
Anthony, Mrs Nellie, Meacham Park
Armstrong, J R, retired, Sappington road
Armstrong, Miss Gussie, Sappington road
Armstrong, Hinton C, physician, Sappington road
Armstrong, Mrs Clara, Sappington road
Aselmann, Wm, blacksmith and wagonmaker, Denny road South Kirkwood
Augusta, Samuel, carpenter, N Cleveland ave
Augusta, Mrs Susie, N Cleveland ave

~ B ~

Bailey, Harris, colored, 314 N Van Buren ave
Bailey, Mrs E, colored, 314 N Van Buren ave
Bailey, Thomas, colored, 314 N Van Buren ave
Baker, Isaac, colored, teamster, 629 E Madison ave
Baker, Mrs Mary, colored, 629 E Madison ave
Baker, J M, Dentist, Agenette ave
Baker, Mrs Madge, Agenette ave
Baker, John, colored, Railroad st near Clay
Baker, Mrs Nellie, colored, Railroad st near Clay
Baker, Joshua, colored, 133 W Madison ave
Baker, Mrs Mattie, colored, 133 W Madison ave
Balch, E A, Insurance, 221 W Way ave
Balch, Mrs Bertha S, 221 W Way ave
Balch, Miss Helen H, 221 W Way ave
Baldenweck, Jos V, salesman, 123 W Clinton ave
Baldenweck, Mrs K, 123 W Clinton ave
Baldenweck, Joseph, salesman, 123 W Clinton ave
Baldenweck, Miss Gertrude, 123 W Clinton ave
Bank of Kirkwood, Webster and Madison aves.
Banks, Geo, colored, Filmore and Madison ave
Banks, Mrs Caroline, colored, Filmore and Madison ave
Barfelt, Mrs Elizabeth, 203a N Webster ave
Barfelt, Miss Freida, 203a N Webster ave
Barfelt, Charles, with Greggís stable, 203a N Webster ave
Barlieh, Melia, maid, 118 W Washington ave
Barnett, Wm, colored, with Beck feed store, 334 Lee ave
Barnett, Mrs Rosetta, colored, 334 Lee ave
Barnett, J W, colored, porter, 225 S Geyer ave
Barnett, Mrs Mattie, colored, 225 S Geyer ave

Barnett, Arthur, colored, 225 S Geyer ave
Barnett, Robert, colored, porter, 225 S Geyer ave
Barr, Miss Bessie, 505 N Webster ave
Barreiras, Julietta, 505 S Clay ave
Barringer, Chas, colored, 228 Bouyer Pl
Barringer, Mrs Chas, colored, 228 Bouyer Pl
Barrington, Mary, colored, servant, 515 N Webster ave
Bass, W H, 417 S Fillmore ave
Bass, Mrs Mary, 417 S Fillmore ave
Bates, Geo H, colored, 625 E Madison ave
Bates, Mrs Mary E, colored, 625 E Madison ave
Bates, Fannie M, colored, 625 E Madison ave
Batson, Jerry, colored, teamster, 638 E Main st
Batson, Mrs Jenne, colored, 638 E Main st
Batson, Kaleb, colored, 413 W Jefferson ave
Batson, Mrs Emma, colored, 413 W Jefferson ave
Becker, Carl, vocal teacher, 473 N Webster ave
Becker, Mrs Margaret E Becker, 473 N Webster ave
Becker, C J, clerck Simmons Hardware Co, 423 W Madison ave
Becker, Mrs L F, 423 W Madison ave
Beckman & Gerfen, Millinery, 202 N Webster ave
Bell, Charley, colored, 341 S Fillmore ave
Bell, Mrs Mary, colored, 641 E Madison ave
Bell, S B, Doctor, colored, 433 S Harrison ave
Bell, Mrs Louise, colored, 433 S Harrison ave
Bell Telephone Co of Mo, 103 East Main st
Bell, Wm, street commissioner, 212 E Jefferson ave
Belt, A R, secíy Lumbermenís Assín, 600 block E Monroe ave
Belt, Mrs L M, 600 block E Monroe ave
Belt, Mrs M A, 468 N Clay ave
Belt, Mrs Mary C, 468 N Clay ave
Bendal, Hulda, maid, 517 S Webster ave
Bender, W T, County School Supít, 5 Hillcrest Pl
Bender, Mrs Rosetta, 5 Hillcrest Pl
Bender, Chas Raymond, bookkeeper Burr Com Agíy, 5 Hillcrest Pl
Bender, Miss Ethel D, teacher, 5 Hillcrest Pl
Benedict, C W, traveling salesman, 110 E Clinton ave
Benedict, Mrs Alice B, 110 E Clinton ave
Benedict, Ruth A, bookkeeper, 110 E Clinton ave
Bennings, Ollie, colored. 655 E Madison ave
Bennett, George, Baker and Confectioner, 203 N Webster ave
Berg & Anth, meat and vegetable market, 209 N Webster ave
Berg, D C, barber, 110 N Webster ave. Res147 W Jefferson ave
Berg, Mrs A, 147 W Jefferson ave
Berg, M F, tinner, Mesker Bros, 419 W Washington
Berg, Mrs M F, 419 W Washington ave
Berg, Mamie, maid, 505 N Taylor ave
Berg, H A, Berg & Anth, 135 E Monroe ave
Berg, Mrs M L, 135 E Monroe ave

Berglund, John, cement work, 737 Cleveland ave
Berglund, Mrs Mary, 737 Cleveland ave
Berthold, F W, retired, Oakwood Hotel
Berthold, J C, Deputy Circuit Clerk, 374 S Taylor ave
Berthold, Mrs H, 374 S Taylor ave
Berthold, Marie, maid, 102 N Taylor ave
Bibb, Susan, colored, 425 W Jefferson ave
Biggs, David, lawyer, 459 N Taylor ave
Biggs, Mrs Alice, 459 N Taylor ave
Biggers, C M, advertising agent, Gill and N Woodlawn
Biggers, Mrs M H, Gill and N Woodlawn
Billings, Geo A, carpenter, 626 E Adams ave
Billings, Mrs I E, 626 E Adams ave
Billings, Myrtle V, 626 E Adams ave
Billings, Geo R, 626 E Adams ave
Bipps, Cornelius, colored, rear 421 S Harrison ave
Bipps, Mrs Nora, colored, rear 421 S Harrison ave
Bird, Mrs Elmira, colored, 125 W Main st
Blackburn, Jasper, mfr Everstick Anchor, 117 E Clinton ave
Blackburn, Mrs Margaret, 117 E Clinton ave
Blackburn, Kate, maid, 142 W Monroe ave
Blankemeier, L, newspaper man, 440 W Madison ave
Blankemeier, Mrs L, 440 W Madison ave
Blankemeier, H, photographic business, 440 W Madison ave
Blankemeier, Miss M, bookkeeper Erker Bros, 440 W Madison ave
Bolard, Andrew, 445 N Harrison ave
Bolard, Mrs A, 445 N Harrison ave
Bolgard, Renard, St Louis Express Co, Heege ave
Bolgard, Mrs Augusta, Heege ave
Bollefer, Mata, domestic, 459 N Taylor ave
Bopp, Andrew, Sr, 439 W Main st
Bopp, Andrew, Jr, 439 W Main st
Bopp, Miss Elizabeth, 430 W Main st
Bopp, Geo, carpenter, 426 W Jefferson ave
Bopp, Mrs W B, 426 W Jefferson ave
Bopp, Gus, carpenter, 409 W Main st
Bopp, Mrs K, 409 W Main st
Bopp, Louis H, Undertaker, 125 W Jefferson ave
Bopp, Mrs F, 121 W Jefferson ave
Bopp, Lula, maid, 418 S Geyer ave
Bopp, Otto, Boots and Shoes, 223 S Webster ave
Bopp, P C, Contractor and Builder, 219 S Webster ave
Bopp, Mrs Emma, 219 S Webster ave
Bopp, Peter, Sr, Boots and Shoes, 223 S Webster ave
Bopp, Mrs A M E, 223 S Webster ave
Bopp, T P W, Architect, 405 W Main st
Bopp, Mrs Mary, 405 W Main st
Bopp, Theo, Contractor and Builder, 108 N Webster ave, Res 403 W Main st
Bopp, Mrs Catherine, 403 W Main st

Bopp, Emil, painter, 403 W Main st
Bopp, Walter, driver, 403 W Main st
Bopp, Valentine, retired, 715 N Harrison ave
Bopp, Mrs Katherine, 715 Harrison ave
Bopp, Valentine, Jr, carpenter, 318 E Adams ave
Bopp, Mrs Louise, 318 E Adams ave
Bopp, Wm, carpenter, 412 W Main st
Bopp, Mrs Cara, 412 W Main st
Borst, Charles A, Aeolian Co, 226 E Main st
Borst, Mrs Agusta, 526 E Main st
Boss, Mamie, maid, 332 W Main st
Bouyer, John, colored, driver, 212 Bouyer ave
Bouyer, Mrs Sarah, colored, 212 Bouyer ave
Bouyer, Franklin, colored, 212 N Woodlawn ave
Bowles, Mrs E E, 735 N Webster ave
Bowles, Margaret, 735 N Webster ave
Bowles, Thomas, 735 N Webster ave
Bowles, Louise, 735 N Webster ave
Bowman, Miss Alice, servant, 217 E Main st
Bowman, Dave, colored, 138 E Monroe ave
Bowman, Mrs Belle, colored, 138 E Monroe ave
Bown, W J H, H & K Coffee Co, 428 S Webster ave
Bown, Mrs M L, 428 S Webster ave
Bown, W T, dealer in Bonds, Leffingwell and Scott ave
Bown, Mrs Victoria, Leffingwell and Scott ave
Boyd, D M, with T B, Boyd F G Co, Woodlawn N of Adams
Boyd, Mrs C J, N Woodlawn ave North of Adams
Boyd, Ingram F, with T B Boyd, 336 N Woodlawn ave
Boyd, Mrs L B, 336 N Woodlawn ave
Boyd, T B, T B Boyd Furnishing Goods Co, N Woodlawn ave
Boyd, Mrs E F, N Woodlawn ave
Boyer, Julia, maid, 316 S Webster ave
Boyer, Mrs Mary, colored, rear 138 E Monroe ave
Boyer, Mollie, colored, rear 138 E Monroe ave
Boyle, Miss F K, servant, 236 E Main st
Bradley, M C, Frav Trt Agt C H & D Ry, Hillcrest Place
Bradley, Mrs Emily S, Hillcrest Place
Bragg, Mrs Emma, Woodlawn Hotel
Branson, Pearl, maid, 422 S Geyer ave
Bredell, Niel, mail carrier, 143 W Jefferson ave
Bredell, Miss May, stenographer, 143 W Jefferson ave
Briggs, John, colored, servant, 453 N Harrison ave
Briggs, Mary, colored, servant, 453 N Harrison ave
Briney, Miss Mary, 123 N Harrison ave
Brinkman, Wm, laborer, N Taylor ave
Brinkman, Mrs Lizzie, N Taylor ave
Brinkman, August, N Taylor ave
Broderick, J K, Brodrick & Bascom, 312 E Jefferson ave
Broderick, Mrs Mabel Bryan, 312 E Jefferson ave

Broeker, Ernest, contractor, 440 S Geyer ave
Broeker, Mrs Emily, 440 S Geyer ave
Brooks, Mrs I B, 505 S Clay ave
Brooks, Geo, colored, 329 S Fillmore ave
Brooks, Mrs Mary, 329 S Fillmore ave
Brossard, Mrs C W, 240 W Main st
Brossard, Miss Julia, 240 W Main st
Brossard, Miss Mary, 240 W Main st
Brossard, Miss Ida, 240 W Main st
Brossard, John, Am. Box Mfg Co, 240 W Main st
Brossard, Miss Cornelia, 240 W Main st
Brossard, J, farmer, Frisco and S Harrison ave
Brossard, Mrs Mary, Frisco and S Harrison ave
Browne, S F, 400 N Taylor ave
Browne, Mrs C, 400 N Taylor ave
Brown, Rev Geo, colored, 638 E Main st
Brown, Mrs Laura, colored, 638 E Main st
Brown, Mrs G L, 114 W Bodley ave
Brown, W C, Ins Agt, 433 S Clay ave
Brown, Mrs Edith, 433 S Clay ave
Brown, M E, 433 S Clay ave
Brown, Ruth F, 433 S Clay ave
Brown, John, 234 E Clinton ave
Brown, Mrs R, 234 E Clinton ave
Brown, G R, carpenter, 451 Van Buren ave
Brown, Mrs P J, 451 Van Buren ave
Brunner, Mrs Ida L, 336 W Madison ave
Brunner, Miss Frances C, teacher, 336 W Madison ave
Brunner, Miss Laura H, music teacher, 336 W Madison ave
Bruner, Mrs S R, 217 E Main st
Bryan, Mrs E J, NE cor Woodlawn and Scott ave
Bryan, Kenneth, NE cor Woodlawn and Scott ave
Bryan, Ben, NE cor Woodlawn and Scott ave
Bryan, Gano, N E cor Woodlawn and Scott ave
Bryant, Mrs Anna, colored, 646 E Main st
Bryant, Ben, colored, rear 421 S Harrison ave
Bryant, Lucinda, colored, rear 421 S Harrison ave
Bryant, C, colored, 622 E Main st
Bryant, Mrs L, colored, 622 E Main st
Bryning, J K, Frisco Agt, S Webster ave
Bryning, Mrs L A, S Webster ave
Buckner, E S, banker, 220 W Washington ave
Buckner, Mrs E T, 220 W Washington ave
Buckner, L W, Bell Tel Co, 220 W Washington ave
Buckner, Mrs Catherine, 220 W Washington ave
Budd, James, gardner, NE cor Essex and Webster ave
Buer, Oscar, painter, 532 Andrews ave
Buer, Mrs Martha, 532 Andrews ave
Burgess, Mrs E, 118 E Clinton ave

Burgess, Miss Florence, 118 E Clinton ave
Burgess, A O, carpenter, 608 S Norton ave
Burgess, Mrs C B, 608 S Norton ave
Bushell, Mrs Margaret, 316 W Sefferson ave
Byars, W V, journalist, 425 N Taylor ave
Byars, Mrs L C, 425 N Taylor ave
Byars, Blanche C, teacher, 425 N Taylor ave
Byars, Mary W, 425 N Taylor ave
Byars, Lucy T, 425 N Taylor ave
Byars, Katherine L, 425 N Taylor ave
Byars, Mildred G, 425 N Taylor ave
Byrd, Schrilda, maid, 303 W Washington ave
Byrd, Mary, maid, 230 W Jefferson ave
Blosser, Gotleib, teamster, 114 W Madison ave
Bishop, L R, 322 N Webster ave

OUTSIDE CITY LIMITS

Backof, Frank, Clerk Frisco, Sappington rd and Sub tracts
Backof, Mrs Mary T, Sappington rd and Sub tracts
Bausch, Christ, stone cutter, N Simmons ave
Bausch, Mrs Agnes, N Simmons ave
Berthold, Wm H, rural postman, N Webster and Wilson aves
Berthold, Mrs Laura, N Webster and Wilson aves
Blake, L, plasterer, Big Bend road
Blake, Wm, plasterer, Big Bend road
Blake, Mrs Clara, Big Bend road
Blakemore, Mrs O, Big Bend road
Boucher, Julius V, Kinloch Tel Co, Parkland Pl, Maple ave
Boucher, Mrs D E, Parkland Pl, Maple ave
Bowline, F M, tel operator, Big Bend road
Bowline, Mrs Lurah, Big Bend road
Britton, F H, E Monroe ave
Britton, Mrs, E Monroe ave
Brooks, Mrs, Parkland Pl, Maple ave
Brook, M M, Parkland Pl, Elm ave
Brown, D S, South Denny road
Brown, Mrs, South Denny road
Braun, Mrs Johana, Peeke ave
Burhen, Jacob, mfr screens, Big Bend road
Burhen, Mrs Mamie, Big Bend road

~ C ~

Cabell, Ashley, lawyer, 613 E Monroe ave
Cabell, Mrs Margaret H, 613 E Monroe ave
Cabell, Miss Margaret, 613 E Monroe ave
Cambrose, Wm, tireman, 726 N Geyer road
Cambrose, Mrs Euna, 726 N Geyer road
Campbell, Miss P M, maid, 109 N Woodlawn ave

Carmen, Chas P, retired chemist, 321 Way ave
Carmen, Mrs Rachel, 321 Way ave
Carpenter, Robt M, carpenter, 614 N Simmons ave
Carpenter, Mrs D M, 614 N Simmons ave
Carriway, Ella, maid, 223 S Woodlawn ave
Carter, E H, 116 W Jefferson ave
Carter, Mrs Jennie, 116 W Jefferson ave
Carter, Mrs Mary, 115 E Washington ave
Carter, Jos, carpenter, 608 Norton ave
Carter, Mrs A C, 608 Norton ave
Carter, Mrs Annie P, 139 W Madison ave
Carter, Edward G, electrician, 139 W Madison ave
Carter, Miss Annie L, teacher, 139 W Madison ave
Carter, Miss Mabel, 139 W Madison ave
Casey, John, colored, 547 S Geyer ave
Caulfield, G W, traveling salesman, 120 W Monroe ave
Caulfield, Mrs T, 120 W Monroe ave
Caulfield, Miss Grace, 120 W Monroe ave
Catlett, Harry C, traveling salesman, 429 W Essex ave
Catlett, Mrs Mary, 429 W Essex ave
Chambers, Ed, colored, 310 Rose Hill ave
Chandler, A B, lawyer, 401 S Webster ave
Chandler, Mrs H, 401 S Webster ave
Chappel, E R, lawyer, 533 E Main st
Chappel, Mrs Esther C, 533 E Main st
Chappel, Banister, colored. catere, 213 S Geyer ave
Chappel, Mrs Lou, 213 S Geyer ave
Chism, Dr, colored, 133 W Main st
Clafhanan, Henry, yardman, 505 N Taylor ave
Claland, Miss N G, 231 W Jefferson ave
Clark, Elijah, colored, 330 Bouyer ave
Clarke, Enos H, lawyer, NE cor Woodlawn and Monroe
Clarke, Mrs M Annette, NE cor Woodlawn and Monroe
Clarke, Miss Rowena A, NE cor Woodlawn and Monroe
Clarkson, Jas D, Real Estate, 315 W Way
Clarkson, Mrs Olive S, 315 W Way ave
Clayton, Rev John B, 425 N Webster ave
Clayton, Mrs Lillie, 425 N Webster ave
Clayton, Miss S S, 425 N Webster ave
Clayton, H Helm, civil engineer, 425 N Webster ave
Clayton, Miss Patti, 425 N Webster ave
Clayton, Miss Francis, 425 N Webster ave
Clement, Chester H, tel operator, 436 Lee ave
Clement, Mrs Rose L, 436 Lee ave
Cochrane, Mrs Theda C, 317 N Woodlawn ave
Cochran, W R, clerk, Pacific Express Co, 128 W Clinton
Cochran, Mrs J, 128 W Clinton
Cole, B L, agent, Arlington Chemical Co, 102 N Taylor ave
Cole, Mrs C A, 102 N Taylor ave

Coleman, Chas H, colored, laborer, 232 Rose Hill ave
Coleman, Mrs Della, 612 N Harrison ave
Coleman, Dan, Meat Market, 127 S Webster
Coleman, Mrs E A, 127 S Webster ave
Coleman, R W, farmer, 528 N Harrison ave
Coleman, Mrs Delia, 528 N Harrison ave
Collier, Clara, maid, 229 Way ave
Collier, John, teamster, 202 S Taylor ave
Collier, Mrs L, 202 S Taylor ave
Collier, Robert, colored, 220 Bouyer Pl
Collier, Mrs Julia, 220 Bouyer Pl
Collins, Miss M, teacher, 448 N Harrison ave
Collins, Robert E, lawyer, 434 E Main st
Collins, Mrs Ida K, 434 E Main st
Compton, Geo P, lithographing, 321 N Harrison ave
Compton, Mrs, 321 N Harrison ave
Compton, R J, lithographing, 135 E Adams ave
Compton, Mrs C L, 135 E Adams ave
Compton, R J Jr, Brokerage, 135 E Adams ave
Conlon, Mrs Mary, 320 W Jefferson ave
Conlon, Miss Mary, 320 W Jefferson ave
Conrad, Ernest A, with Bradstreet, 217 E Main st
Conway, Wm, Concrete, Tile Roofing, 222 E Main st
Conway, Mrs Margaret O, 222 E Main st
Conway, Harold, 222 E Main st
Conway, Miss Lutie, 222 E Main st
Cook, Newton, laborer, 242 Rose Hill ave
Cook, Mrs Hugusta, 242 Rose Hill ave
Cook, Mrs Ellen, colored, 310 Rose Hill ave
Cooper, Mart, 556 S Clay ave
Cooper, Mrs, 556 S Clay ave
Cooper & Havermale, agts, Singer Sewing Machines, 113 W Main st
Corbyn, Henry Sr, Insurance, 321 W Main st
Corbyn, Marmaduke, insurance, 321 W Main st
Corbyn, Henry Jr, with D R Francis, 408 W Main st
Corbyn, Mrs Maud, 408 W Main st
Corley, John, retired, 422 S Geyer ave
Corley, Mrs Catherine, 422 S Geyer ave
Corley, John, Fidelity Storage Co, 422 S Geyer ave
Corley, Joseph, Bridge & Beach, 422 S Geyer ave
Corley, Louis, 422 S Geyer ave
Corley, Thos W, law reporter, 418 S Geyer ave
Corley, Mrs N, 418 S Geyer ave
Corley, Millard Harper, Brown Shoe Co, 418 S Geyer ave
Corley, Daniel, clerk Edgar Zinc Co, 418 S Geyer ave
Corley, Claiborne, clerk, Frisco, 418 S Geyer ave
Corley, Harry C, Brown Shoe Co, 431 S Geyer ave
Corley, Mrs M B, 431 S Geyer ave
Corley, Ed, colored, 224 Bouyer ave

Corley, Mrs Ethel, colored, 224 Bouyer ave
Cornell, Abigail, servant, 316 N Taylor ave
Coutler, Jos. Hay, Grain, Flour, 113 N Webster ave, Res 123 W Madison ave
Coutler, Mrs E L, 123 W Madison ave
Coutler, Mrs E, 123 W Madison ave
Courier The, newspaper, S J Harris, prop, 208 N Webster ave
Craig, Lallie, maid, Clinton and S Webster ave
Crashaw, Mrs Laura F, 428 N Taylor ave
Cronin, M W, Hardware. Stoves, Tinware, 136 S Webster, Res 370 S Webster ave
Cronin, Mrs D, 370 S Webster ave
Cronin, Mrs Julia, 370 S Webster ave
Cropper, Mrs Mary, colored, rear 421 S Harrison ave
Crosby, Ben G, St Louis Cordage Co, N Taylor ave
Crosby, Mrs E P, N Taylor ave
Crosby, H W, Norvel Shapleigh, 303 W Washington ave
Crosby, Mrs H E, 303 W Washington ave
Crow, O R, clerk Mars & Lautz, 120 S Harrison ave
Crow, Mrs L M, 120 S Harrison ave
Crowder, J W, veterinary surgeon, 132 E Monroe ave
Crowder, Mrs J, 132 E Monroe ave
Crowson, F H, carpenter, 116 S Harrison ave
Crowson, Mrs S E, 116 S Harrison ave
Crutsinger, H J, Insurance, 418 S Clay ave
Crutsinger, Mrs B M, 418 S Clay ave
Crutsinger, R W, city collector, 418 S Clay ave
Crutsinger, R M, 418 S Clay ave

OUTSIDE CITY LIMITS

Calvert, E L, merchant, S Denny road
Calvert, J B, merchant, S Denny road
Calvert, Mrs E K, S Denny road
Calvert, Mrs M H, S Denny road
Chambers, Jerome, Sappington road
Colus, Miss L, Parkland Pl, Maple ave.
Courtney, M, Saloon, S Denny road
Courtney, Mrs E, S Denny road
Cowling, Richard, stair builder, Meacham Pk, New York st
Cowling, Mrs Ida, Meacham Pk, New York st
Curlee, J R, E Monroe ave
Curlee, Mrs, E Monroe

~ D ~

Dahl, Mary, maid, 237 W Washington ave
Daly, W M, Plumbing, Stoves and Tinware, 153 W Main st, Res 220 W Main st
Daly, Mrs N, 220 W Main st
Daly, Miss Rose, 103 N Harrison ave
Dana, Miss Virginia, 302 W Main st
Dana, Miss Leslie, Mfg Stoves and Ranges, 344 W Main st
Dana, Mrs C, 344 W Main st

Darley, R M, asst engineer, Burlington, 421 N Webster ave
Darley, Mrs Harriett E, 421 N Webster ave
Darley, Lucile, 421 N Webster ave
Darnell, colored, 126 W Jefferson ave
Darnell, Mrs Amy, 136 W Jefferson ave
Davidson, A R, bookkeeper, S Leffingwell ave
Davidson, Mrs Grace, S Leffingwell ave
Davis, A J, bond dealer, 225 W Jefferson ave
Davis, Mrs A J, 225 W Jefferson ave
Davis, Adams, W Washington and Geyer aves
Davis, Mrs Jane, W Washington and Geyer aves
Davis, Mrs C L, teacher, 306 S Webster ave
Davis, Carroll W, Bank Commerce, 202 E Adams ave
Davis, Mrs Ruth B, 202 E Adams ave
Davis, Earl, colored, blacksmith helper, 442 W Adams ave
Davis, Olvina, colored, plasterer, 442 W Adams ave
Davis, Ethel, maid, 124 E Adams ave
Davis, Geo, colored, plasterer, 442 W Adams ave
Davis, Mrs Grace, 442 W Adams ave
Davis, M, engineer Mo Pac, 114 W Madison ave
Davis, Miranda, 413 S Geyer ave
Davis, Ernest, 413 S Geyer ave
Davis, Mrs Jane, colored, Mo P tracks and Geyer ave
Davis, Mrs Nelson, 573 S Geyer ave
Davis, Miss Elizabeth Nelson, 573 S Geyer ave
Davis, Irvin, acountant, 573 S Geyer ave
Davis, Theodre, colored, 310 Rose Hill ave
Davis, Elanor, colored, 310 Rod Hill ave
Davis, M B, plasterer, 442 W Adams ave
Davis, Mrs L, 442 W Adams ave
Davison, Wm J, Kirkwood Ice & Fuel Co, 132 E Monroe ave
Davison, Mrs Jennie, 132 E Monroe ave
Day, Richard M, dealer commercial paper, 325 N Dickson
Day, Lydia P, 325 N Dickson st
Deacon, R F, Printing & Stationery, 622 E Monroe ave
Deacon, Mrs E A, 622 E Monroe ave
DeBerard Jr, salesmanager, 645 N Taylor ave
DeBerard Jr, Mrs Lucreti, 645 N Taylor ave
DeFlorin, F J, Contractor Brick Work, 127 E Monroe ave
DeFlorin, Mrs A K, 127 E Monroe ave
DeFoe, Miss F E, 448 N Harrison ave
DeHoog, Girard, Coal & Building Material, 122 S Webster ave, Res 202 S Taylor ave
DeHoog, Mrs S R, 202 S Taylor ave
DeHoog, Miss Charlotte, elocutionist, 202 S Taylor ave
DeHoog, Rudolph, tinner, 202 S Taylor ave
Denny, Frank G, tinner, Heege ave
Denny, Mrs Margaret, Heege ave
Devolt, Jas, laborer, Frisco and S Harrison ave
Devolt, Mrs L, Frisco and S Harrison ave

Dickmann, Carrie maid, 505 N Taylor ave
Dieter, J H, Sligo Iron Co, 126 E Bodley ave
Dieter, Mrs A E, 126 E Bodley ave
Dietleman, Henry, tinner, 317 W Essex ave
Dietleman, Mrs, 317 W Essex ave
Dionysius, Henry J, Dr, 125 E Adams ave
Dionysius, Mrs L E, 125 E Adams ave
Dionysius, Louis P, 125 E Adams ave
Dionysius, Mary J, 125 E Adams ave
Dobbins, Wm, 575 W Monroe ave
Dodge, Frank M, retired farmer, 520 E Adams ave
Dodge, Mrs R, 520 E Adams ave
Doebler, Chas, wood worker, 521 W Washington ave
Doebler, Mrs, 521 W Washington ave
Doerr, Alexander, 460 N Clay ave
Doerr, Mrs Anna, 460 N Clay ave
Doerr, Oscar, carpenteer, 457 S Harrison ave
Doerr, Mrs Katie, 457 S Harrison ave
Doerr, George, contractor, 521 S Geyer road
Doerr, Mrs, 521 S Geyer road
Dohr, Fred, mgr Hough Realty Co, 611 E Jefferson ave
Dohr, Mrs Kate, 611 E Jefferson ave
Dohr, Albert F, with Hough Realty Co, 611 E Jefferson ave
Dohr, Miss Mabel J, 611 E Jefferson ave
Dohr, Carl, janitor, 2d floor, 111 W Madison ave
Domrese, Gus, driver, 115 E Monroe ave
Domrese, Mrs E, 115 E Monroe ave
Domrese, Chas, clerk, 438 S Harrison ave
Domrese, Mrs Mary, 438 S Harrison ave
Donahoe, Miss Nellie, servant, 306 N Woodlawn ave
Donaldson, M J, 131 E Monroe ave
Donaldson, Flora, maid, 131 E Monroe ave
Donaldson, Hulda, maid, 131 E Monroe ave
Donaldson, Chas, tinner 131 E Monroe ave
Donaldson, Clarence, driver, 131 E Monroe ave
Donovan, Douglas, R R Contr, 456 N Webster ave
Donovan, Mrs Bessie, 456 N Webster ave
Donovan, Harry D, Bank of Kirkwood, 456 N Webster ave
Donovan, Douglas H, 456 N Webster ave
Donovan, Miss Bessie, 456 N Webster ave
Donworth, Wm, tinner, Furnaces, Stoves, 204 N Webster ave, res 233 W Jefferson ave
Donworth, Mrs C D, 233 W Jefferson ave
Doran, Mrs Mary, N E corner Woodlawn and Monroe ave
Dorn, Miss Emily, Jefferson and Fillmore ave
Dorris, Mr B E, Oakwood Hotel, Webster and Adams ave
Dorris, Mrs, Oakwood Hotel, Webster and Adams ave
Dorsch, Martha, 344 W Main st
Douglas, R, Ins Agt, 215 S Webster ave
Douglas, Mrs E, 215 S Webster ave

Douglas, Rufus, 326 Rose Hill ave
Dunbar, C N, with Simmons Hdw. Co, 432 N Van Buren ave
Dunbar, Mrs M H, 438 N Van Buren ave
Duncan, J T, laborer, Midway ave near Clay ave
Duncan, Mrs May, Midway ave near Clay ave
Dunham, Fred, plasterer, 207 S Geyer ave
Dunn, Maria, colored, 423 W Jefferson ave
Dunn, Andrew, colored, 423 W Jefferson ave
Dunn, Martha, colored, 423 W Jefferson ave
Dunnavant, C A, physician, 109 E Jefferson
Dunnavant, Mrs Mary E, 109 E Jefferson
Dunnavant, Miss Virginia, teacher, 431 N Van Buren ave
Dupy, Docer, colred, 622 E Main st
Dupy, Mrs A, colored, 622 E Main st
Durand, Mrs Annie, 217 S Geyer ave
Durand, Felix, tinner, 217 S Geyer ave
Durand, Ed, tinner, 217 S Geyer ave
Durfee, B E, carpenter, 415 S Van Buren ave
Durfee, Mrs J, 415 S Van Buren ave
Dussing, Geo P, retired, 515 S Webster ave
Dussing, Mrs K L, 515 S Webster ave
Dwyer, P J, liveryman, N Webster ave
Dwyer, Mrs Anne, N Webster ave

OUTSIDE CITY LIMITS

Daegele, Edward, butcher, N Evans ave
Daegele, Mrs Elizabeth, N Evans ave
Denniston, Chas C, Pacific Exp, Edwin ave, Parkland Pl
Denniston, Mrs T M, Edwin ave, Parkland Pl
Devlin, Hugh, liquor compounder, N Cleveland ave
Devlin, Mrs Margaret, N Cleveland ave
Dice, Walter C, asst cashier St L P O, Sappington near Main
Dice, Mrs I G, Sappington road near Main
Dickey, Chas, laborer, N Evans ave
Dickey, Mrs Laura, N Evans ave
Dickson, E P, Sappington road
Dorsey, M L, granitoid worker, N Simmons ave
Dorsey, Mrs Margaret L, N Simmons ave
DuBois, Milton, contractor, 824 N Harrison ave
DuBois, Mrs Martha, 824 N Harrison ave
DuBois, Miss Eva, 824 N Harrison ave
Dusard, Mrs Marie L, Sappington and Sub tracks
Dusard, Mrs Marie A, Sappington and Sub tracks

~ E ~

Eastman, Louis, watchman Mo Pac, 120 W Madison ave
Eastman, Mrs C, 120 W Madison ave
Edgerton, Mrs M, 135 E Washington ave
Edmund, Mrs Jane, 223 W Van Buren ave
Edwards, A N, lawyer, 517 S Webster ave

Edwards, Mrs S H, 517 S Webster ave
Edwards, George Lane, Broker, 516 S Webster ave
Edwards, Mrs F N, 516 S Webster ave
Edwards, Geo Locket, lawyer, 535 S Webster ave
Edwards, Mrs Jett, 535 S Webster ave
Edwards, J H, florist, 538 N Harrison ave
Edwards, Mrs A, 538 N Harrison ave
Edwards, Mrs Lucy, colored, 122a W Jefferson ave
Edwards, Nathan, colored, W Washington ave and Geyer road
Edwards, Mrs Clara, W Washington ave and Geyer road
Edwards, N G, Secíy Kenard Carpet Co, 528 E Monroe ave
Edwards, Mrs E C, 528 E Monroe ave
Edwards, Mrs H J, 528 E Monroe ave
Edwards, Miss Constance, 528 E Monroe ave
Edwards, Miss Harriet, 528 E Monroe ave
Edwards, Murray, teacher, 528 E Monroe ave
Edwards, Mrs Sarah J, 127 W Adams ave
Edwards, W J, florist, 751 N Woodlawn ave
Edwards, Mrs Anna A, 751 N Woodlawn ave
Edwards, Miss Pearl, 751 N Woodlawn ave
Edwards, Miss Stella, 751 N Woodlawn ave
Eickman, Louis, 121 W Jefferson ave
Eigenbrod, Andrew, bricklayer, 445 S Harrison ave
Eigenbrod, Mrs Ida, 445 S Harrison ave
Elmer, Chas F, letter carrier, 118 S Harrison ave
Elmer, Mrs S T, 118 S Harrison ave
Engler, John, painter, 438 S Clay ave
Engler, Albert, trav salesman, 438 S Clay ave
Engler, Mrs Sophia, 438 S Clay ave
Engler, Miss Cornelia, 438 S Clay ave
Erker Bros, Opticians, Photo Supplies, 604 Olive St., St. Louis
Eslemoien, Maggie, maid, 502 S Webster ave
Eslemont, Mary, maid, 535 S Webster ave
Essex, Mrs E B, 428 N Taylor ave
Etts, Realty Co, Edgar P Holly, manager, 2nd floor, 105 N Webster ave
Evans, Mrs H C, 516 S Webster ave
Evans, Mrs H DeF, 303 W Washington ave
Evans, Walker H, Cíwealth Steel Co, 303 W Washington ave
Evans, Miss Marion V, nurse, 303 W Washington ave
Evans, Mrs Lizzie, 120 W Madison ave
Evans, Lee Walker, Arts and Crafts Goods, 114 N Webster
Everett, Miss Lou, 307 S Webster ave
Ewald, J Howard, Ewald Iron Co, 238 W Washington ave
Ewald, Mrs M, 238 W Washington ave
Ewing, Fayette C, throat and ear specialist, 402 S Woodlawn
Ewing, Mrs Martha M, 402 S Woodlawn ave
Ewing, Fayette C, Jr, 402 S Woodlawn ave
Ewing, E M, 402 S Woodlawn ave
Ewing, Presley K, 402 S Woodlawn ave

Ewing, Donnell M, 402 S Woodlawn ave
Ewing, Wm, Gardner, 505 N Taylor ave
Ewing, W K, commission merchant, 519 S Clay ave
Ewing, Mrs Mary E, 519 S Clay ave
Ewing, Miss Jessie, stenr Meyer Boiler Works, 519 S Clay ave
Ewing, Mrs Mary, 519 S Clay ave

OUTSIDE CITY LIMITS

Eime, Henry, painter, S Denny and Brooklyn aves
Eime, Mrs Josephine, S Denny and Brooklyn aves
Eime, Mrs Wm, S Denny and Brooklyn aves
Ellis, W C, decorator, Maple ave, Parkland Pl
Ellis, Mrs L J, Maple ave, Parkland Pl
Ellis, S R, Thread Agent, Edwin ave, Parkland Pl
Ellis, Mrs C M, Edwin ave, Parkland Pl
Engel, Geo, with Wagner Electrical Co, Meacham Park
Engel, Mrs K, Meacham Park
Engle, Alfred N, leather dealer, N Webster ave
Engle, Mrs A F, N Webster ave
Evans, L W, Elm ave, Parkland Pl
Evans, Mrs M A, Elm ave, Parkland Pl

~ F ~

Faerber, Arthur, florist, 604 Evans ave
Faerber, Mrs Mary, 604 Evans ave
Fahrin, Rose, maid, 516 S Webster ave
Fantroy, Dena, colored, 417 W Jefferson ave
Fantroy, Wm, colored, 140 E Monroe ave
Fantroy, Ida, colored, 140 E Monroe ave
Farmer, Jos, carpenter, Clinton and Fillmore aves
Farmer, Mrs Helen, Clinton and Fillmore aves
Farrington, Henry P, Texas Land Agent, 332 W Main st
Farrington, Mrs E B, 332 W Main st
Farris, F P, 139a S Webster ave
Farris, Mrs M J, 139a S Webster ave
Farris, J C, retired liveryman, 130 W Jefferson ave
Farris, Mrs Eva, 130 W Jefferson ave
Faser, Fred, restaurant keeper, Leffingwell and Elliot aves
Faser, Mrs Sophia, Leffingwell and Elliot aves
Fasnauch, Miss Elsa, 307 S Webster ave
Fedder, Albert, St Louis P O, 139 W Bodley ave
Fedder, Mrs K, 139 W Bodley ave
Ferguson, Mrs Angelo, colored, 428 S Harrison ave
Field, A L, Oakwood Hotel
Fielding, O, retired, 110 E Clinton ave
Fields, Mrs Anna, colored, 642 E Main st
Fight, Mrs F J, 338 E Adams ave
Fight, F J, clerk Wabash, 338 E Adams ave

Fight, Estella, 338 E Adams ave
Finlay, Jas W, with Waters Pierce Oil Co, 615 E Jefferson ave
Finlay, Mrs Grace L, 615 E Jefferson ave
Fischer, Mrs L, 213 W Main st
Fischer, Frank, 213 W Main st
Fishback, John, colored, porter Mo Pac, 6 Sante ave
Fishback, Mrs S A, 6 Sante ave
Fishback, Mrs Sarah, colored, cook, Washington and Fillmore ave
Fiske, Geo F, Treas Am Stove Co, 306 N Woodlawn ave
Fiske, Mrs Mary Z, 306 N Woodlawn ave
Fiske, Miss Harriet P, 306 N Woodlawn ave
Fister, Jos, clerk, 434 W Madison ave
Fister, Mrs C C, 434 W Madison ave
Fitzgerald, Patrick, tireman Mo Pac, 325 W Woodbine ave
Fitzgerald, Mrs Lena, 325 W Woodbine ave
Flint, Mrs, colored, 445 W Jefferson ave
Flint, Riley, colored, 447 W Jefferson ave
Flint, Mary, colored, 447 W Jefferson ave
Flournoy, Miss Ethelene, teacher, 230 East Main st
Floyd, G G, Am Steel Foundry Co, 235 E Jefferson ave
Floyd, Mrs Mabel, 235 E Jefferson ave
Foley, Daniel, retired, 742 N Webster ave
Foley, Mrs B, 742 N Webster ave
Follett, Walter, Oakwood Hotel
Follett, Mrs Jessie, Oakwood Hotel
Ford, Eva, colored, servant, 515 N Webster ave
Forrester, Thos, retired, 651 E Monroe aves
Forrester, Mrs, 651 E Monroe ave
Forrester, Richard, retired, 651 E Monroe ave
Forrester, Mrs A R, 651 E Monroe ave
Forrester, Arthur D, 651 E Monroe ave
Forsyth, Robt, physician, 120 N Harrison ave
Forsyth, Mrs Bettie, 120 N Harrison ave
Forsyth, Mrs L P, 453 N Harrison ave
Foster, Geo, paper and painting, 745 N Simmons ave
Foster, Mrs Hattie, 745 N Simmons ave
Fortune, Miss Carrie, 213 S Clay ave
Fortune, Carroll, retired, 213 S Clay ave
Fortune, Mrs Ella E, 213 S Clay ave
Francis, John, machimist, 440 Rose Hill ave
Francis, Mrs Marie, 440 Rose Hill ave
Frankenstein, Henry, Tailor, 150 W Main st
Franklin, Miss Mary, 621 E Monroe ave
Franklin, Miss Laura, 621 E Monroe ave
Franklin, Miss Alice, 621 E Monroe ave
Freeman, Mrs Mary, 307 S Webster ave
French, Jesse R, Pac Exp Co Aud office, 217 E Main st
French, Mrs Lillian B, 217 E Main st
Friel, Mrs Jane, 307 W Essex ave

Fuchs, Agnes, domestic, 302 E Adams ave
Fuchs, Josephine, 742 N Webster ave
Fulkerson, Ben, with Bradstreet, 513 N Clay ave
Fulkerson, Mrs Ben, 513 N Clay ave
Fulkerson, W P, with Bradstreet, 131 W Bodley ave
Fulkerson, Mrs K M, 131 W Bodley ave
Funk, Daniel J, retired, Essex and N Taylor aves
Funk, Mrs Mary T, Essex and N Taylor aves
Funk, Clifford B, contractor, Essex and N Taylor aves
Funk, Daniel R, Essex and N Taylor aves
Funk, Neil James, Essex and N Taylor aves
Funk, Robt A, Essex and N Taylor aves
Fuszner, Miss Julia M, domestic, 512 N Taylor ave
Fuszner, Lizzie Z, domestic, 459 N Taylor ave
Fyfe, Miss G, maid, 505 N Taylor ave

OUTSIDE CITY LIMITS

Fritsch, Joseph, barber, N Cleveland ave
Fritsch, Mrs Anna, N Cleveland ave
Forrester, Mrs M, Edwon ave, Parkland Pl
Forrester, Jewell, Edwon ave, Parkland Pl

~ G ~

Gains, Ed, colored, 312 W Clinton ave
Gains, Mrs Jane, colored, 312 W Clinton ave
Gallop, James, 109 W Jefferson ave
Galloway, Julia, colored, rear 409 S Harrison ave
Gardner, A E L, lawyer, 243 W Jefferson ave
Gardner, Mrs Adelaibe, 243 W Jefferson ave
Gardner, Cora Lee, teacher, 116 N Taylor ave
Gardner, O G, lumberman, Oakwood hotel
Gardner, Mrs L L, proprietress Oakwood Hotel
Garner, A R, colored, 316 N Van Buren ave
Garner, Mrs M Belle, colored, 316 N Van Buren ave
Gauss, Edward, teamster, 114 W Madison ave
Gayer, Hy J, clerk, 439 W Main st
Gayer, Mrs Catherine, 439 W Main st
Geiger, Elsie, maid, 215 N Taylor ave
Geiger, John, 475 S Harrison ave
Gaiger, Mrs Josephine, 475 S Harrison ave
George, Mrs E,324 W Madison ave
Gerould, Mrs H B, 231 W Jefferson ave
Gerringer, Minnie, servant, 345 W Main st
Ghiselin, Horace, 242 W Adams ave
Ghiselin, Mrs E W, 242 W Adams
Gholson, Thomas, colored, 11 Santa ave
Gholson, Mrs Ellen, 11 Santa ave
Gholson, Mrs Etta, 11 Santa ave
Gibbons, Dan, boss yard gang Mo Pac, rear 202 S Taylor ave
Gilgen, Helen, 340 E Main st

Gill, Harry B, retired, 429 E Main st
Gill, Mrs Adelina, 429 E Main st
Gill, Mrs Ellen B, 429 E Main st
Gillham, S S, farmer, 615 E Jefferson ave
Gillham, Mrs L M, 615 E Jefferson ave
Githens, J N, Gen Frt Agt Mo Pac, 134 E Adams ave
Githens, Mrs Elizabeth B, 134 E Adams ave
Godefried, yardman, 742 N Webster ave
Goericke, Chas, shoemaker, 224 S Geyer road
Goericke, Mrs Elizabeth, 224 S Geyer road
Goericke, Otto, painter, 224 S Geyer road
Goericke, Fred, painter, 224 S Geyer road
Goericke, Chas, stonemason, 240 S Geyer road
Goltz, Emil, 403 W Main st
Good, M S, W Washington ave
Good, Mrs Josephine, W Washington ave
Goodin, Wm, 325 S Fillmore ave
Goodin, Mrs Mamie, 325 S Fillmore
Gordan, Mrs Bessie, colored, 213 S Geyer ave
Gordon, Agnes, maid, 535 S Webster ave
Gorman, J D, commission agt, Abbett Addition S Mo Pacific
Gorman, Mrs C F, Abbett Addition S Mo Pacific
Gorman, C F, Supt Crescent Lead & Oil Co, Abbett Addition S Mo Pacific
Gorman, J D, med student, Abbett Addition S Mo Pacific
Gorman, Miss M Elizabeth, Abbett Addition S Mo Pacific
Gott, F J, Agt Nat Life Ins Co, 312 N Clay ave
Gott, Mrs M C, 312 N Clay ave
Gottlieb, Julia, 440 N Van Buren ave
Gottlieb, Mrs Emma, 440 N Van Buren ave
Gratz, Anderson, E Bodley ave
Gratz, Mrs Laura, E Bodley ave
Gratz, Miss Katherine, E Bodley ave
Gray, John L, contractor, 317 N Woodlawn ave
Gray, Mrs Elizabeth G, 317 N Woodlawn ave
Gray, Edward L, Mo Pac R R, 317 N Woodlawn ave
Gray, Karl L, clerk, 317 N Woodlawn ave
Gray, Edith J, 317 N Woodlawn ave
Gray, H J, colored, 340 S Fillmore ave
Green, A P, Fire Brick Mfr, 330 E Main st
Green, Jos B, 330 E Main st
Green, Mrs Caroline, 324 W Jefferson ave
Green, Howard, clerk, 324 W Jefferson ave
Green, Mrs M A, 307 S Webster ave
Green, Mrs Martha, 341 S Fillmore ave
Greenburg, Samuel, merchant, 450 S Geyer ave
Greenburg, Mrs Anne, 450 S Geyer ave
Greenburg, Miss Bora, 450 S Geyer ave
Greensfelder, J B, capitalist, 109 N Woodlawn ave
Greensfelder, Mrs Sarah, 109 N Woodlawn ave

Greensfelder, Harry, physician, 109 N Woodlawn ave
Gregg, Geo H, Livery and Feed Stable, 125 127 W Jefferson ave, Res 436 N Clay ave
Gregg, Mrs E A, 436 N Clay ave
Gregg, Alvin, 436 N Clay ave
Gregg, Harold, 436 N Clay ave
Gregg, Miss Myrtle, 436 N Clay ave
Grieger, Louise, cook, 507 N Taylor ave
Griffin, David, colored, 333 S Fillmore ave
Griffin, Mrs Bell, colored, 333 S Fillmare
Griffith, Mrs Mary, 118 W Washington ave
Griffith, Miss, teacher, 118 W Washington ave
Grissom, D M, 307 S Webster ave
Gristwalc, Christ, carpenter, 629 E Main st
Gristwalc, Margaret, 629 E Main st
Grochan, F X, title examiner, 213 S Clay ave
Grochan, Mrs N, 213 S Clay ave
Grocock, Albert I, salesman, 302 E Adams ave
Grocock, Mrs F, 302 E Adams
Gross, Mrs Aliza, 401 S Geyer ave
Gudermuth, Miss Louise, 109 E Jefferson ave
Gunn, Mrs M C, 230 W Washington ave
Gunn, Miss L K, 230 W Washington ave
Gurney, Robt, Commonwealth Trust Co, 125 E Woodbine ave
Gurney, Mrs Grace, 125 E Woodbine

OUTSIDE CITY LIMITS

Gassner, John, laborer, Big Bend Road
Gassner, Mrs C, Big Bend rd
Gieseking, Henry, retired, 811 N Harrison ave
Gieseking, Mrs Minnie, 811 N Harrison ave
Gieseking, Henry F W, gardener, 811 N Harrison ave
Gillock, Conrad, N Evans ave
Gillock, Mrs Amelia, N Evans
Goss, John C, huckster, N Simmons ave
Goss, Mrs Theresa, N Simmons
Grant, Geo C, Shoe Mfr, Edwin ave, Parkland Pl
Grant, Mrs Geo C, Edwin ave, Parkland Pl
Griffeth, M W, traveling salesman, 825 N Harrison ave
Griffeth, Mrs Flora, 825 N Harrison
Grosscop, H, Brick contractor, Edwin ave, Parkland Pl
Grosscop, Mrs, Edwin ave, Parkland Pl
Grossgloss, Wm, with D Prough & Son, Meacham Park
Grossgloss, Mrs A, Meacham Park

~ H ~

Haberle, Chas F, painter, S Taylor ave
Haberle, Mrs G, S Taylor ave
Haberle, Miss Hulda, teacher of piano, S Taylor ave
Hagleman, Henry, 530 S Fillmore ave

Hagleman, Mrs Marthe, 530 S Fillmore ave
Haight, Col, E A, Kirkwood Military Acdy, Washington and Fillmore ave
Haight, Mrs L C, Washington and Fillmore ave
Haight, Edward A, 483 N Webster ave
Haight, Mrs Edward A, 483 N Webster ave
Hakuba, Mrs S, servant, 102 N Taylor ave
Hall, A E, Lincoln & Pope, Alice ave & Mo Pac
Hall, Mrs Lillie, Alice ave & Mo Pac
Hall, Jas J, carpenter, 303 W Essex ave
Hall, Mrs Emma, 303 W Essex ave
Hallison, Chas, colored, 364 S Fillmore ave
Hameister, H M, agt Mo Pac, 332 S Webster ave
Hameister, Mrs C, 332 S Webster ave
Hameister, Fannie, 332 S Webster ave
Hamilton, Chas, with Bank of Commerce, 230 W Washington ave
Hamilton, Mrs M K, 230 W Washington ave
Hamilton, E A, contractor, 116 S Harrison ave
Hamilton, Miss Ola, tel operator, 116 S Harrison ave
Hamilton, Jas, carpenter, 646 Cleveland ave
Hamilton, Mrs Blanche, 646 Cleveland ave
Hamilton, John F, carpenter, 721 Simmons ave
Hamilton, Mrs Cora, 721 Simmons ave
Hamilton, J J, with Cupples W w Co, 135 E Washington ave
Hamilton, Mrs Lucy K, 135 E Washington ave
Hamilton, W S, Granitoid cont, 719 N Evans ave
Hamilton, Mrs Lola, 719 N Evans ave
Hammel, Leana, maid, 529 N Clay ave
Hanson, John, plasterer, 308 E Adams ave
Hanson, Mrs Christina, 308 E Adams ave
Hansen, L P, plasterer, 728 Cleveland ave
Hansen, Mrs J E, 728 Cleveland ave
Hanson, Nels, hod carrier, 114 W Madison ave
hanson, Robt, Contíng Plasterer, 737 Simmons
Hanson, Mrs W E, 737 N Simmons ave
Harbour, W C, painter, 125 E Monroe ave
Harbour, Mrs M J, 125 E Monroe ave
Harbour, C W, painter, 125 E Monroe
Hard, M E, Supít Kirkwood school, 116 N Taylor ave
Hard, Mrs Catherine S, 116 N Taylor
Hard, Miss Nora E, 116 N Taylor
Hard, Miss Anita, teacher, 116 N Taylor
Hardeck, Minnie, maid, 237 W Adams ave
Hardt, E J, Groceries and Meats, 554 N Harrison
Hardt, Mrs E, 554 N Harrison ave
Hargis, Jennie, maid, 302 W Main st
Harper, Frank, colored, 364 S Taylor ave
Harper, Mrs Mary W, 126 E Bodley ave
Harper, J R, Mo Pac office, 118 W Madison ave
Harper, Mrs I F, 118 W Madison

Harper, J W, bookkeeper, 117 W Madison ave
Harper, Mrs L D, 117 W Madison ave
Harper, Charles, Traffic Inspection Bureau, 117 W Madison
Harper, Frank, Pacific Exp Co, 117 W Madison
Harper, W, driver Bopp, 206 W Main st
Harper, Mrs, 206 W Main st
Harris, F D, Meats and Vegetables, 203 S Webster ave, Res 110 E Madison ave
Harris, Mrs Agnes, 110 E Madison ave
Harris, Henry, retired farmer, 705 N Taylor ave
Harris, Mrs Katherine, 705 N Taylor ave
Harris, Otto, butcher, 705 N Taylor ave
Harris, Martin, butcher, 705 N Taylor
Hawken, J G, lawyer, 414 E Madison ave
Hawken, Mrs Kate L, 414 E Madison ave
Hawken, Chas C, civil engineer, 414 E Madison ave
Hawken, Eugene W, saleman Cort, Silk Co, 414 E Madison ave
Hawken, Thos M, rec clerk F & S, 414 W Madison ave
Hawkins, Mrs Lizzie, colored, 421 S Geyer road
Hawkins, Hattie, colored, 421 S Geyer road
hartman, Geo F, florist, 751 N Dickson st
Harvey, Mrs Emma, colored, 364 S Taylor ave
Harvey, J C, 237 W Washington ave
Harvey, Mrs J A, 237 W Washington ave
Harvey, Miss A G, 237 W Washington ave
Harvey, Miss L A, 237 W Washington ave
Harvey, Sam, colored, laborer, 641 E Madison ave
Harvey, Mrs Emma, colored, 641 E Madison ave
Harrison, C J, lawyer, 600 S Fillmore ave
Harrison, Mrs L, 600 S Fillmore ave
Harris, S J, publisher The Courier, 461 N Clay ave
Harris, Mrs C J, 461 N Clay ave
Harris, Miss Ruth Jane, 461 N Clay ave
Hayden, Bert, 421 S Fillmore ave
Hayden, Mrs Missouri, 421 S Fillmore ave
Hayes, Wm E, night marshal, 242 W Woodbine ave
Hayes, Mrs M, 242 W Woodbine ave
Hayes, Woodus, teacher, 242 W Woodbine ave
Hayes, W T, colored, janitor, 326 E Main st
Hayes, Mrs Emma, colored, 326 E Main st
Hays, Geo C, carpenter, 450 S Harrison ave
Hays, Mrs P G, 450 S Harrison ave
Hazard, N, retired, Scott and Clarke aves
Hazard, Rebecca N, Scott and Clarke aves
Hazard, Grace, Scott and Clarke aves
Hazenstab, J A, photos, 2nd floor 209 N Webster ave
Heatherly, Mrs Kate, colored, 328 S Taylor ave
Heaton, Miss Isabelle, teacher, 135 E Washington ave
Heege, August, Heege Grocery Co, Webster and Madison aves
Heege, Mrs A, Heege Grocery Co, Webster and Madison aves

Heege, Fred, Heege Grocery Co, 221 S Webster ave
Heege, Mrs R, 221 S Webster ave
Heege, Theo, General Merchandise, Webster and Madison aves, Res 315 S Clay ave
Heege, Mrs Johanna, 315 S Clay ave
Heidbredder, Chas W, retired, 738 N Geyer road
Heidbredder, Mrs M, 738 N Geyer road
Heidorn, Mrs E A, 406 N Taylor ave
Heidorn, Miss Anna, 406 N Taylor ave
Heinzelmann, Leo E, General Mdse and Meats, 155-159 W Main st
Heinzelman, Mrs Lula Jewel, 155 W Main st
Hellinghoff, Katie, domestic, 127 E Main st
Hemm, Mrs Caroline C, 529 N Clay ave
Henderson, H M, salesman, 243 E Main st
Henderson, Mrs Laura P, 243 E Main st
Henry, Mrs Rosetta, colored, 670 E Main st
Hensick, Wm, carpenter, 522 N Harrison ave
Hensick, Mrs Clara, 522 N Harrison ave
Hepps, Frank, painter, 120 W Madison ave
Hepps, Mrs Maud, 120 W Madison ave
Herman, Geo B, civil engineer, 201 N Dickson st
Herman, Mrs Gertrude, 201 N Dickson st
Herpst, Louis, laborer, 347 Rose Hill ave
Herpst, Mrs Elizabeth, 347 Rose Hill ave
Herpst, Olive, 347 Rose Hill ave
Herpst, Edward, with Kennard & Son, 347 Rose Hill ave
Hesse, Mary, 344 W Main st
Hester, J C, salesman, 127 E Jefferson ave
Hester, Mrs Mary W, 127 E Jefferson ave
Hickman, Clement S, with Kernard & Son, 525 E Main st
Hickman, Mrs Celeste, 525 E Main st
Hickman, F M, treas Mo Pac, 209 W Adams ave
Hickman, Mrs J, 209 W Adams ave
Hickman, B F, 209 W Adams ave
Higgenbotham, Hy, lawyer, 214 S Clay ave
Higgenbotham, Mrs Mary V, 214 S Clay ave
Hill, Dr H M, 143 W Clinton Pl
Hill, Mrs M C, 143 W Clinton Pl
Hill, S L, with Banner Lum Co, Woodbine and Magnolia aves
Hill, Mrs Emily, Woodbine and Magnolia aves
Hilton, Fred, concrete worker, 705 N Taylor
Hilton, Mrs Anna, 705 N Taylor
Hoemann, R H, jeweler, 727 N Evans ave
Hoemann, Mrs L B, 727 N Evans ave
Hodge, Miss Julia M, teacher, 315 W Adams ave
Hodges, Mrs Belle, 207 S Geyer road
Hodges, Amos C, 207 S Geyer road
Holden, Thomas, painter, 228 E Clinton Pl
Holden, Mrs Addie, 228 E Clinton Pl
Holekamp Lumber Co, R E Holekamp, Mgr, 113 E Main st

Holladay, Stafford, colored, 322 S Taylor ave
Holladay, Mrs N, 322 S Taylor ave
Hollenbeck, Eugene, 143 W Jefferson ave
Hollman, Louis, postal clerk, 135 E Clinton Pl
Hollman, Mrs Lizzie, 135 E Clinton Pl
Hollman, Fred, 364 S Fillmore ave
Hollopeter, R E, mail carrier, 123 N Harrison ave
Hollopeter, Mrs Florence reed, 123 N Harrison ave
Holly, Edgar P, lawyer, 105 N Webster ave, Res 133 W Clinton
Holly, Mrs Annie M, 133 W Clinton Pl
Holmes, Mrs E L, 432 N Van Buren ave
Holmes, Miss Bertha, teacher, 432 N Van Buren ave
Holt, Laura, domestic, 428 N Taylor ave
Holt, J J, laundry, Menken and N Simmons aves
Holt, Mrs Rosa, Menken and N Simmons aves
Holtzman, J H, clerk Mo Pac, 127 E Jefferson ave
Hornbrook, John, Carnegie Steel Co, 135 E Washington ave
Hornbrook, Mrs Gertrude, 135 E Washington ave
Hough, Henry W, Secy School Board, N E cor Essex and Webster aves
Hough, Mrs Ella Cecil, Essex and Webster
Hough, Wm E, with Lambert Pharmacal Co, Essex and Webster
Hough, Emmeline R, Essex and Webster
Hough, Jessie B, teacher, Essex and Webster
Hough, Mrs Ellen S, 410 N Taylor ave
House, Ben, Harrison and Lee ave
House, Mrs Ben, Harrison and Lee ave
Houston, Edward, colored 334 S Fillmore ave
Houston, Mrs Mary L, 334 S Fillmore ave
Howard, Volma, colored, Woodlawn Hotel
Howell, Fred, contractor and Builder, 105 W Main st, Res 653 Evans ave
Howell, Mrs Agnes, 653 Evans ave
Howell, J, decorator, 105 W Main st, Res 425 S Van Buren ave
Howell, Mrs M, 425 S Van Buren
Howell, Willie, 425 S Van Buren
Howell, John, contractor, 230 W Adams ave
Howell, Mrs M, 230 W Adams ave
Howell, Miss Ada E, 230 W Adams
Howell, R W, N E cor Woodlawn and Monroe aves
Hoyt, F W, Jeweler, 334 S Clay ave
Hoyt, Mrs M A, 334 S Clay
Hubbard, J C, 579 W Monroe ave
Hubbard, Mrs Hattie, 579 W Monroe
Huckeby, R G, carpenter, Woodbine and Andrews aves
Huckeby, Mrs J M, Woodbine and Andrews aves
Huckins, C M, traveling salesman, 229 W Adams
Huckins, Mrs A G, 229 W Adams ave
Hudgens, J B, plasterer, 207 S Geyer ave
Hudgens, Mrs Clara B, 207 S Geyer ave
Hudgins, Alonzo, 346 S Fillmore ave

Hudgins, Mrs Mary, 346 S Fillmore ave
Huellingshoff, Mary, domestic, 240 E Main st
Hughes, J N, retired farmer, 444 N Webster ave
Hughes, Mrs F L, 444 N Van Buren ave
Hughes, Joseph N, real estate 455 N Webster ave
Hughes, Mrs Sarah, 455 N Webster ave
Hughes, Mrs M E, rear 439 N Clay ave
Hull, O Sr, retired engineer, 202 N Taylor ave
Hull, Mrs H, 202 N Taylor ave
Hull, O Jr, with Union Electric Co, 122 E Jefferson ave
Hull, Mrs E, 122 E Jefferson ave
Hunkler, Tillie, 507 N Taylor ave
Hunt, A C, clerk Pac Exp Co, 402 W Main st
Hunt, Mrs A, 402 W Main st
Hunter, John, colored, carpenter, Fillmore and Mo Pac
Hunter, Mrs Hattie, Fillmore and Mo Pac
Hunter, Shed, Fillmore and Mo Pac
Hunter, Mrs Della, Fillmore and Mo Pac
Hupp, T J, 210 N Clay ave
Hupp, Mrs S L, 210 N Clay ave
Hurstcamp, Hy J, carpenter, 223 S Webster ave
Hurstcamp, Mrs Louise, 223 S Webster ave
Husband, Mrs E J, 132 W Main st
Huston, Jacob P, retired, 414 S Clay ave
Huston, Mrs Kate, 414 S Clay ave
Hutchinson, Wm, florist, 344 S Webster ave
Hutchinson, Mrs M A, 344 S Webster ave
Hutchinson, E M, 344 S Webster ave
Hutton, S S, brakeman Mo Pac, 124 W Madison ave
Hutton, Mrs K, 124 W Madison ave
Hyatt, Mrs H A, 433 S Webster ave
Hyatt, Edward, civil engineer, 432 S Webster ave
Hyatt, Harry H, 359 S Webster ave
Hyatt, Mrs Frances, 359 S Webster ave

OUTSIDE CITY LIMITS

Hacbarth, O G, Parkland Pl
Hacbarth, Mrs Nannie H, Parkland Pl
Hamilton, T E, granitoid worker, N Cleveland ave
Hamilton, Mrs Bertha, N Cleveland
Harrison, A J, concrete worker, N Evans ave
Harrison, Mrs Mary, N Evans ave
Hayhurst, J S, clerk St L P O, W Washington ave
Hayhurst, Mrs H, W Washington
Hayhurst, Miss R L, W Washington
Hayhurst, Miss E, W Washington
Heidel, August, Meacham Park
Heidel, Mrs Josephine, Meacham Park
Heidel, Mrs Elizabeth, Meacham Park

Hickman, Vaughan, E Monroe ave
Hickman, Mrs, E Monroe
Holscher, Edward A, salesman, Parkland Pl
Holscher, Mrs Hortense, Parkland Pl

~ J ~

Jaccaty, John A, printer, 456 N Clay ave
Jaccaty, Mrs Maria L, 456 N Clay ave
Jacobi, H S, Justice of the Peace, 6 Hillcrest Pl
Jacobi, Miss Ida, 6 Hillcrest Pl
Jacobi, Chas A, solicitor Bell Tel Co, 6 Hillcrest Pl
Jacobs, Anna, maid, 115 E Woodbine ave
Jackson, Abraham, colored, janitor, 611 Cleveland ave
Jackson, Mrs Ida, colored, 611 Cleveland
Jackson, E A, colored, 219 N Van Buren ave
Jackson, Mrs Bessie, colored, 219 N Van Buren ave
Jackson, Mrs T, colored, 632 E Main st
Jackson, Wm, colored, 217 Bouyer ave
Jackson, Mrs Clara, colored, 217 Bouyer
James, J T, lawyer, 111 N Harrison ave
James, Mrs M L, 111 N Harrison ave
Jenkins, Rev L R, pastor M E church, 521 N Clay ave
Jenkins, Mrs M H, 521 N Clay ave
Jenkins, Miss Mary Ruth, nurse, 239 Way ave
Jenkins, Wm H, colored, boiler cleaner, 731 N Harrison ave
Jenkins, Mrs Carrie, colored, 731 N Harrison ave
Johnson, Miss Annie, 505 S Clay ave
Johnson, B H, coffee merchant, 203 S Woodlawn ave
Johnson, Mrs E F, 203 S Woodlawn
Johnson, Benjamin, colored, 673 E Madison
Johnson, Mrs Cloren, colored, 673 E Madison
Johnson, Mrs Bettie, colored, 318 S Taylor ave
Johnson, G W, contíg carpenter, 135 W Monroe ave
Johnson, Mrs E L, 135 W Monroe
Johnson, Jas W, colored, 670 E Main st
Johnson, Mrs Mary E, colored, 670 E Main st
Johnson, Louis, electrician, 364 S Taylor ave
Johnson, Mrs Margaret, 451 N Taylor ave
Johnson, Miss Blanche, 451 N Taylor
Johnson, Mary, maid, 608 E Monroe ave
Johnson, Ollie, colored, maid, 223 S Woodlawn ave
Johnson, Rachel, colored, 205a N Van Buren ave
Jones, Arthur, Steel Foundry, 314 Rose Hill ave
Jones, Mrs E, 314 Rose Hill ave
Jones, Annie, colored, servant, 325 W Washington ave
Jones, Collins, colored, janitor, 435 S Fillmore ave
Jones, Mrs Lena, 435 S Fillmore
Jones, E F B, Cordage Co, 512 N Taylor ave
Jones, Mrs Cecil B, 512 N Taylor ave

Jones, Ellis, colored, 338 W Washington ave
Jones, Mrs E T, colored, 338 W Washington
Jones, Harriet, colored, 325 S Fillmore ave
Jones, James, plasterer, 269 S Geyer ave
Jones, Mrs Mamie, 209 S Geyer
Jones, J M, carpenter, 424 Lee ave
Jones, Mrs M C, 424 Lee ave
Jones, E O, Paper Hanger & Painter, 424 Lee ave
Jones, John, S Webster ave near Frisco
Jones, John, colored, 443 W Jefferson ave
Jones, Mrs Delia, 443 W Jefferson ave
Jones, Capt L F, banker, 505 N Taylor ave
Jones, Mrs M F, 505 N Taylor ave
Jones, F M, 505 N Taylor ave
Jones, Miss M F, 505 N Taylor ave
Jones, L F Jr, 507 N Taylor
Jones, Mrs Elizabeth W, 507 N Taylor ave
Jones, Wm, colored, 326 Lee ave
Jones, Mrs, colored, 326 Lee ave
Jurden, Clyde W, Banner Lumber Co, 479 N Webster ave
Jurden, Mrs Elizabeth, 479 N Webster

OUTSIDE CITY LIMITS

Jones, S E, traffic man John Deer Plow Co, Parkland Pl
Jones, Mrs Grace, Parkland Pl

~ K ~

Kadelburg, F e, Broker, 218 N Dickson st
Kadelburg, Mrs Clementin, 218 N Dickson st
Kaflich, Amelia, maid, 502 S Webster ave
Kolmbacker, Mrs M, 543 W Monroe st
Kane, Mrs M A, 329 W Main st
Kane, Michael, teamster, 329 W Main st
Kane, Miss N G, stenographer, 329 W Main st
Kean, Franklin, prof W U, 243 W Main st
Kean, Mrs Maud, 243 W Main st
Keck, Adam, stonemason, 720 Cleveland ave
Keck, Mrs Minnie, 720 Cleveland ave
Keelan, Owen, Loborer, 424 S Van Buren ave
Keelan, Mrs Kate, 424 S Van Buren ave
Kelly, d, Plumber, 204 N Webster ave, Res 419 W Mian st
Kelly, Jas, rr watchman, 419 W Main st
Kelly, Mrs Catherine, 419 W Main st
Kelly, Michael, 419 W Main st
Kelly, Bridget, 419 W Main st
Kelly, James Jr, bookkeeper, 419 W Main
Kelly, Wm, plasterer, 419 W Main
Kelly, John, baker, 419 W Main
Kelton, J L, retired, 509 N Van Buren
Kelton, Jas W, 509 N Van Buren

Kelton, Mrs Mary A, 509 N Van Buren
Kelton, Miss Mary A, 509 N Van Buren
Kelton, T L, with T B Boyd, 331 Way ave
Kelton, Mrs J W, 331 Way ave
Kern, Mrs E, 455 N Clay ave
Kern, Miss J E, 455 N Clay
Kern, R S, 455 N Clay
Kerth, CP, 135 W Washington ave
Kerth, Mrs J E, 135 W Washington ave
Kerth, Geo & Sons, Mercantile Co, Adams and Webster aves
Kerth, Geo, 127 W Washington ave
Kerth, Mrs C F, 127 W Washington ave
Kerth, Miss E R, 127 W Washington ave
Kerth, Lewis J, 127 W Washington ave
Kerth, Geo F, 239 W Way ave
Kerth, Mrs L F, 239 W Way
Kessler, Alex, capitalist, 432 N Clay
Kessler, Mrs M E, 432 N Clay ave
Kessler, Wm G, carpenter, 701 Evans ave
Kessler, Mrs Anna, 701 N Evans
Kettler, Hy, stonemason, 525 S Geyer ave
Kettler, Mrs Margaret, 525 S Geyer
Key, Geo, fireman, Monroe and Harrison aves
Key, Mrs N, Monroe and Harrison
Key, T Ed, engineer, Fillmore and Clinton
Key, Mrs Martha J, Fillmore and Clinton
Keysor, W W, Prof W U, 122 N Fillmore
Keysor, Mrs J E, 122 N Fillmore
Keysor, H C, 122 N Fillmore
Keysor, W E, 122 N Fillmore
King, Miss Caroline M, teacher, 331 E Main st
King, E C, dealer in bonds, 630 E Monroe ave
King, Mrs A, 630 E Monroe ave
King, Ed R, postal clerk, 7 Hillcrest Pl
King, Mrs Ida B, 7 Hillcrest Pl
King, Norwood, clerk, 219 E Washington ave
King, Miss Lillie, bookkeeper, 219 E Washington
King, Mrs Minnie, 219 E Washington ave
King, Wullus S, retired, 240 E Main st
King, Mrs Lucy G, 240 E Main st
King, Katherine G, teacher, 240 E Main st
King, Benjamin A, with Burr & Co, 240 E Main st
Kingdon, Mrs Wm, 406 N Taylor ave
Kingland, Walter, salesman, 225 E Clinton Pl
Kingland, Mrs, 225 E Clinton Pl
Kimball, Clinton, Cordage Co, 220 W Washington ave
Kimball, Mrs A B, 220 W Washington
Kimball, T D, agt Wash Life Ins Co, 127 E Main st
Kimball, Mrs Belle C, 127 E Main st

Kinkead, J H, salesman, 124 N Taylor ave
Kinkead, Mrs Jennie, 124 N Taylor
Kinkead, Maud A, teacher, 124 N Taylor
Kinkead, Virginia H, 124 N Taylor
Kinkead, Lois, 124 N Taylor
Kinkead, Gordon F, salesman, 124 N Taylor
Kinkead, T J, traveling salesman, 124 N Taylor
Kinkead, Mrs M B, 111 N Harrison
Kinkead, Miss Mary, 11 N Harrison
Kinkead, Ed R, Editor Kirkwood Tablet, 109 N Webster ave
Kinsella, P J, 541 N Clay ave
Kinsella, Mrs M H, 541 N Clay
Kinsella, Miss Genevieve, 541 N Clay
Kinyon, A S, Coal Ice and Wood, S Webster & Frisco aves
Kinyon, Mrs M E, 326 Rose Hill
Kirk, Donnell, teacher, Oakwood Hotel
Kirkwood Ice & Fuel Co, 145 W Main st
Kirkwood Laundry Co, 132-136 E Madison ave, B E Dorris, manager
Kirkwood Military Academy, Col E A Haight, Washington & Fillmore aves
Kirkwood Planing Mill, E Monroe bet Taylor and Fillmore aves
Kirkwood Printing & Publishing Co, publishers of the Kirkwood Tablet, 109 N Webster, Ed
    R Kinkead, Mgr
Kirkwood Trust Co, Main and Webster aves
Kiskaddon, J C, lawyer, 241 W Adams ave
Kiskaddon, Mrs M M, 241 W Adams ave
Kiskaddon, A H, 241 W Adams ave
Klamberg, Fred, model maker, 440 Lee ave
Klamberg, Mrs Pauline, 440 Lee
Klinger, Louise, maid, 243 W Main st
Klingsick, Edward, Painter, 229 S Van Buren ave
Klingsick, Mrs Fredericke, 229 S Van Buren
Knapp, C L, with Pacific Express Co, 108 N Taylor ave
Knapp, Mrs B F, 108 N Taylor
Knapp, Alice M, 108 N Taylor
Knierim, J H, Meat Market, 102 N Webster ave, Res 449 N Clay ave
Knierim, Mrs Clara, 449 N Clay
Knierim, Wm, city inspector, 426 N Webster ave
Knierim, Mrs J E, 426 N Webster ave
Knott, E W, 207 E Jefferson ave
Knott, Mrs, 207 E Jefferson ave
Kopp, Alois, servant, 302 W Main st
Kottwitz, Lizzie, 113 W Jefferson
Krieager, Mary, maid, Gill & Woodlawn aves
Kuhn, Augusta, maid, 434 N Harrison ave
Kuehnle, Erick, chemist, Woodlawn Hotel
Kullmar, J F, Harness, 115 N Webster ave, Res 321 Menken ave
Kullmar, Mrs Mary, 321 Menken
Kullmar, John F Jr, stereotyper, 649 N Harrison ave
Kullmar, Mrs Anna, 649 N Harrison

OUTSIDE CITY LIMITS

Keisker, Otto, Parkland Place
Keisker, Mrs, Parkland Place
Kinnear, G H, Thread Agcy, Parkland Place
Kinnear, Mrs Guy, Parkland Place
Kley, Mrs Katherine, Meacham Park
Klene, Wm, real estate, Sappington road
Klene, Mrs M G, Sappington road
Knott, Miss S, maid, Denny road & Manchester
Kuhn, Julius, paper hanger, Meacham Park
Kuhn, Mrs Berhtha, Meacham Park

~ L ~

Lackey, Wm G, Miss, Valley TrustCo, 222 E Jefferson ave
Lackey, Mrs Rose, 222 E Jefferson ave
Laderle, John, 116a W Jefferson ave
Laderle, Mrs Catherine, 116a W Jefferson ave
Lake, Miss Margie, 505 S Clay ave
Lamoureux, D A, retired lumberman, 322 N Webster ave
Lamoureux, Josephine, 322 N Webster ave
Landers, Mrs Sarah M, 331 E Main st
Landers, Miss Francis M, 331 E Main st
Landers, Miss Caroline M, 331 E Main st
Landl, Gottleib, retired, 537 W Washington ave
Landl, Mrs Rosa, 537 W Washington
Landon, Mrs Carrie, colored, 319 Rose Hill ave
Landon, Chas, 319 Rose Hill
Landvatter, Geo Sr, retired, 701 N Evans ave
Lane, Dennis, watchman, 211 S Taylor ave
Lane, Mrs B, 211 S Taylor
Lane, Nora, 211 S Taylor
Lane, Agnus, 211 S Taylor
Lane, James, 211 S Taylor
Lautermilch, Chester Harry, painter, 221 S Geyer ave
Lautermilch, Mrs Agusta, 221 S Geyer
Lautermilch, John, painter, 221 S Geyer
Lautermilch, Fred, painter, 233 E Clinton Pl
Lautermilch, Mrs Mary, 233 E Clinton Pl
Lauts, Geo laborer, 439 S Harrison ave
Lauts, Mrs Geo, 439 S Harrison
Lautz, F E, Mars & Lautz, 118 E Jefferson ave
Lautz, Mrs Elizabeth H, 118 E Jefferson ave
Lawton, Chas A, 338 W Main st
Lawton, Mrs L E, 338 W Main
Lear, R H, carpenter and builder, 330 E Adams ave
Lear, Mrs C M, 330 E Adams
Lear, Mrs A S, 330 E Adams
Leary, Mrs Mary, 239 S Van Buren ave

Lee, Mrs Linda, colored, 330 S Taylor ave
Leet, M W, insurance, 306 S Webster ave
Leet, Mrs E H, 306 S Webster ave
Leet, Frank, insurance, 547 S Webster
Leet, Mrs, 547 S Webster
Leegendre, insurance, Woodlawn Hotel
Lelley, Mrs M M, 437 N Clay ave
Lelley, Miss Leorna E, 437 N Clay
Lelley, Miss June L, 437 N Clay ave
Lemmie, Isaac, janitor, 207 Rose Hill ave
Lemmie, Mrs Alice, 207 Rose Hill ave
Lemmie, Ruby, 207 Rose Hill ave
Lenz, Chas, Blacksmith, 218 N Clay ave
Lenz, Mrs Eda, 218 N Clay
Lenz, Fred, blacksmith, 114 W Madison ave
Leuthauser, Mrs C K, Midway ave near Clay
Leuthauser, J E, driver, Midway ave near Clay
Leuthauser, J M, carpenter, 342 Lee ave
Leuthauser, Mrs Elizabeth, 342 Lee ave
Leuthauser, Fred M, painter, 342 Lee ave
Leuthauser, John E, driver Weber Grocery Co, 342 Lee ave
Leuthauser, K E, 342 Lee ave
Lowell, Mrs Mary, colored, 207 N Jefferson ave
Lewis, J B, retired farmer, 431 N Van Buren ave
Lewis, Mrs Mary E, 431 N Van Buren ave
Leykam, Frances, maid, 516 S Webster ave
Leykam, John, landscape gardener, 434 S Taylor ave
Leykam, Mrs L, 434 S Taylor ave
Lintner, H H L, 464 N Clay ave
Lintner, Mrs A N L, 464 N Clay ave
Leippelman, Mrs Charlotte, 138 W Clinton Place
Leippelman, Miss Orlinda, 138 W Clinton Place
Lippelt, Mrs H K, 117 N Harrison ave
Lippelt, Miss Marie H, 117 N Harrison ave
Liseur, (Mr and Mrs) Abbett addition, Southwest Kirkwood
Little, R E, farmer, 518 S Geyer road
Little, Mrs Mary E, 518 S Geyer road
Lloyd, Emil J, Mo Pac Shops, 418 S Taylor ave
Lloyd, Mrs J M, 418 S Taylor ave
Lloyd, A L, 418 S Taylor ave
Lobinger, Jennie, servant, 330 E Main st
Lockhause, John J, carpenter, 627 N Harrison ave
Lockhause, Mrs Kate, 627 N Harrison ave
Lockhause, Paul, blue prints, 627 N Harrison ave
Loren, K, colored, laborer, 213 S Geyer road
Lowber, Fredík, salesman, 429 N Webster ave
Lowber, Mrs M E, 429 N Webster ave
Lowe, R E, railway mail clerk, 324 W Madison ave
Lucas, Frank Jr, tinner, 409 W Woodbine ave

Lucas, Mrs Catherine, 409 W Woodbine
Lucas, Frank M, gardner, 618 E Adams ave
Lucas, Mrs Mary C, 618 E Adams ave
Lucas, Miss Margaret, bookkeeper, 618 E Adams
Luepken & Migneron, Grocers, 100 N Webster
Luepken, H J, Luepken & Migneron, 324 E Adams ave
Luepken, Mrs Mary, 324 E Adams
Luepken, Miss Teckla, 324 E Adams
Lycett, E H, aud Mo Pac, 440 S Webster ave
Lycett, Mrs Anna F, 440 S Webster ave
Lycett, Helen M, 440 S Webster ave
Lycett, Rebecca A, 440 S Webster ave
Lycett, Geo R, civil engineer, 440 S Webster ave
Lyons, Catherine, servant, N Woodlawn ave
Lyons, Mrs G H, 448 N Clay ave
Lyons, James E, colored, 750 N Taylor ave
Lynch, Hugh, brakeman Mo Pac, Essex ave, W of Geyer
Lynch, Mrs Jas, Essex w of Geyer
Lynch, Miss Mary, Essex w of Geyer
Lynch, John, nachinist, 316 W Jefferson ave
Lynch, Mrs Catherine, 316 W Jefferson ave
Lynch, (Mr and Mrs), Oakwood Hotel
Lynch, Miss Margaret, Oakwood Hotel

OUTSIDE CITY LIMITS

Lewis, Alex P, carpenter, Meacham Park
Lewis, Mrs Mary A, Meacham Park
Lewis, Elwood, Meacham Park
Lewis, Irl, Lippencott Mfg Co, Denny & Big Bend roads
Lewis, Mrs Josephine, Denny & Big Bend roads
Lindsay, C B, tariff ins, Main and Sappington roads
Lindsay, Mrs L, Main and Sappington
Lindsay, Miss Eugenia, Main and Sappington
Locke, Mrs Elizabeth E, North Harrison ave
Logan, Hugh, traveling salesman, Parkland Place
Logan, Mrs Emma, Parkland Place
Logan, George, newspaper man, Parkland Place

~ M ~

Mabrey, T W, clerk Custom House, 631 E Jefferson ave
Mabrey, Mrs Anna M, 631 E Jefferson
Mack, H E, 226 Way ave
Mack, Mrs A, 226 Way
Mack, Miss Mildred, 226 W Way
Mack, Bertram, 226 W Way
Madison, Levi, colored, 124 W Jefferson ave
Madison, Mrs Minnie, colored, 124 W Jefferson
Madison, Harry, colored, 124 W Jefferson
Madison, Rosie, colored, 124 W Jefferson

Mansfield, Mrs Josephine, cook, Woodlawn & Monroe
Mardaus, Miss Nellie, 444 N Clay ave
Mardaus, Henry, 444 N Clay
Mardaus, Mrs Annie E, 444 N Clay
Marks, Mr and Mrs, 20 Santa ave
Mars, W T, Kirkwood Trust Co, 324 N Taylor ave
Mars, Mrs Laura, 324 N Taylor
Mars & Lautz, Druggists, 105 N Webster ave
Martin, Geo C Jr, 241 E Main st
Martin, Mrs Louis Northrup, 241 E Main
Martin, J E, broker, 315 S Woodlawn ave
Martin, Mrs J E, 315 S Woodlawn
Martin, R T, ins agt, 323 S Webster ave
Martin, Mrs A B, 323 S Webster
Marvin, engineer Mo Pac, 517 W Washington ave
Marvin, Mrs Mary J, 517 W Washington ave
Marvin, Ohmer, 517 W Washington
Marvin, Geo W, brakeman Mo Pac, 450 N Harrison ave
Marvin, Mrs E, 450 N Harrison
Massey, Joseph, colored,122 W Jefferson ave
Massey, Belle, colored, 122 W Jefferson
Massey, Lavina, colored, 122 W Jefferson
Massey, Sidney, colored, 122 W Jefferson
Masters, Brant, hostler, Mo Pac, 119 E Monroe ave
Masters, Mrs L M, 119 E Monroe
Masters, Margaret, housegirl, 119 E Monroe
Masters, C F, painter, 481 S Van Buren ave
Masters, Mrs R E, 481 S Van Buren
Matthews, John O, Bank of Commerce, 441 S Webster ave
Matthews, Mrs C L, 441 S Webster
Matthews, Joseph R, Mational Oats Co, 479 N Taylor ave
Matthews, Mrs Charlotte, 479 N Taylor
May, A W, carpenter, 639 N Evans ave
May, Mrs Flora, 639 N Evans
McAnally, Mrs L E, 117 E Clinton Pl
McCarthy, Mrs Frances A, 118 W Monroe ave
McCarthy, John, clerk, 119 W Monroe
McClure, Mrs M, 114 W Madison ave
McColloh, S H, lineman, 109 W Jefferson ave
McColloh, Mrs J R, 109 W Jefferson
McCollough, Edward E, 139 W Madison ave
McCollough, Mrs Margaret, 419 S Van Buren ave
McCollough, Catherine, 419 S Van Buren ave
McCollough, Thos J, conductor Mo Pac, 423 Van Buren ave
McCollough, Mrs L F, 423 S Van Buren
McCollough, M F, 423 S Van Buren
McCollough, Benj H, clerk, 423 S Van Buren
McConnell, Mrs Mary, Woodlawn Hotel
McCrackin, E Y, Prescription Druggist, 126 S Webster ave, Res 359 S Taylor ave

McCrackin, Mrs Lillie, 359 S Taylor ave
McCray, Estelle, colored, maid, 600 block E Monroe
McDonald, Eli, colored, Taylor and Monroe
McDonald, Mrs Eva, Taylor and Monroe
McDonald, Jas, carpenter, Heege ave
McDanald, Mrs Rose, Heege ave
McDonald, T D, electrician, 117 E Monroe ave
McDonald, Mrs M, 117 E Monroe
McDonnell, F M, ast acct Mo Pac, 437 W Main st
McDonnell, Mrs Genevieve, 437 W Main
McDonnell, Martin, r car insp, Mo Pac, 112 Railroad st
McDonnell, Mrs M R, 112 Railroad st
McDonnell, Ed, plumber, 112 Railroad
McDonnell, R, 112 Railroad
McDonnell, Rose, 112 Railroad
McDermott, Hugh, Mo Pac, 114 E Madison ave
McDermott, Mrs L, 114 E Madison ave
McElroy, John A, 525 E Main st
McElroy, Mrs Fannie M, 525 E Main st
McEnnis, Michael, cor Gill & Fillmore aves
McEnnis, Michael Jr, cor Gill & Fillmore aves
McFarland, J A, colored, houseman, Scott & Holmes ave
McGarty, M C, mail carrier, 444 N Harrison ave
McGee, Mrs Jennie, colored, 326 Rose Hill ave
McGerdy, Hugh, colored, rear 421 S Harrison ave
McGinnis, Wm, laborer, 424 S Van Buren ave
McGinnis, Thomas, laborer, 424 S Van Buren
McGirk, I A, bank clerk, 211 W Jefferson ave
McGirk, Mrs, 211 W Jefferson
McGrath, P J, stonemason, 627 N Cleveland ave
McGrath, Mrs Sarah, 627 N Cleveland
McKee, John, merchant, 232 Way ave
McKee, Mrs F, 232 Way
McKee, John Jr, salesman, 232 Way
McKelvey, John, coal & moving, 116 E Jefferson ave
McKelvey, Mrs Addie L, 116 E Jefferson
McKelvey, J H, with Laclede-Christy Co, 116 E Jefferson
McKelvey, Edith A, teacher, 116 E Jefferson
McLean, C H, pres McLean Med Co, 345 E Main st
McLean, Mrs M, 345 E Main
McLean, Mrs Luytie E, 124 N Taylor ave
McLean, Mrs Mary, 547 S Geyer ave
McLean, Miss Elvira, 547 S Geyer
McMillan, Thos, comm merchant, 303 Way ave
McMillan, Mrs E W, 303 Way
McMillan, Miss Dorris, 303 Way
McMillan, Norman H, Am Met Co, 303 Way
McMillan, Douglas, Yonn & Erber Co, 303 Way
McMullen, P J, cashier Bank of Kirkwood, 230 W Monroe ave

McMullen, Mrs, 230 W Monroe
McMullen, Mrs Mary, 202 W Monroe
McMullen, Mamie, 202 W Monroe
McMullen, Kate, clerk Bank of Kirkwood, 202 W Monroe
McMullen, Nannie, 202 W Monroe
McMullen, Nellie, teacher, 202 W Monroe
McMullen, Gertrude, 202 W Monroe
McRoberts, Mrs Elspeth, 128 W Clinton Place
Means, Phillip, colored, 533 W Monroe ave
Means, Mrs Mamie, 533 W Monroe
Medearis, C W, traveling salesman, Woodlawn Hotel
Medearis, Mrs Emma, Woodlawn Hotel
Medearis, Edgar Dean, Woodlawn Hotel
Meeks, F K, Wholesale Dry Goods, 216 E Main st
Meeks, Mrs J F, 216 E Main st
Meeks, Geo K, Wholesale Dry Goods, 216 E Main st
Mendham, J R, engineer, 220 Way ave
Mendham, Mrs A L, 220 Way
Mendham, Chas Thomas, 220 Way
Mendham, Miss Nillie M, 220 Way
Metcalf, Geo C, Pac Exp Co, 602 S Geyer ave
Metcalf, Mrs, 602 S Geyer
Metropolitan Life Insurance Co, Leegendre, GV, mgr, 103 W Main st
Metzler, Mrs Phoebe, 138 W Clinton Place
Meyers, Matilda, domestic, 118 E Bodley ave
Meyer, Soloman, 109 N Woodlawn ave
Meyer, Mrs Ella, 109 N Woodlawn
Michel, E A, Florists, Geyer & Rose Hill ave
Michel, Mrs A A, Geyer & Rose Hill
Michel, A A, Geyer & Rose Hill
Migneron, Louis, Luepken & Migneron, 628 N Cleveland ave
Migneron, Mrs Annie, 628 N Cleveland
Miller, Chas, lithographer, 114 W Bodley ave
Miller, Mrs M B, 114 W Bodley ave
Miller, Crume K, Notary Public, 218 N Dickson st
Miller, Mrs Helen L, 218 N Dickson
Miller, Robert, hired man, 202 S Taylor ave
Miller, Hugh, tinner, 230 E Clinton Place
Milz, Florence, maid, 305 N Harrison ave
Ming, Freeman, colored, 214 Bouyer ave
Ming, Chas L, colored, laborer, 232 Rose Hill ave
Ming, Mrs Elizabeth, colored, 232 Rose Hill
Mitchell, Miss Ella, 328 W Jefferson ave
Mitchell, James, colored, steel worker, 309 S Taylor ave
Mitchell, Mrs Meda, 309 S Taylor ave
Mitchell, O E, rear 439 N Clay ave
Mitchell, Mrs Wm, rear 439 N Clay
Mitchell, W L, rear 439 N Clay
Mitchell, L, rear 439 N Clay

Mitchell, Z J, lawyer, 211 N Taylor ave
Mitchell, Lizzie, 211 N Taylor
Mitchell, Irwin G, lawyer, 211 N Taylor
Moeller, agt Polar Wave, Fillmore & Monroe aves
Moeller, Mrs L, driver, Fillmore & Monroe
Maule, Geo F, driver, 122 W Adams ave
Maule, Mrs Sarah, 122 W Adams
Monnier, Miss Ida L, 132 W Main st
Monroe, Mrs Sarah, colored, 232 Rose Hill ave
Moore, Frank, rear 316 W Clinton Place
Moore, Mrs J, rear 316 W Clinton
Moore, John, clerk, 155 W Main st
Moore, Mrs Matilda, 155 W Main
Moore, John R, r r clerk, 211 E Jefferson ave
Moore, Mrs Fannie B, 211 E Jefferson
Moore, Louis D, Scientific Illuminating, 211 E Jefferson
Morrill, C H, indust agt Frisco, 220 W Monroe ave
Morrill, Mrs A F, 220 W Monroe
Morrill, Mildred, 220 W Monroe
Morrill, Hazel, 220 W Monroe
Morrill, Mrs and Miss Nellie, Oakwood Hotel
Morris, E K, hardware, 545 S Geyer ave
Morris, Mrs Emma, 545 S Geyer
Mortensen, F H, laborer, 230 E Clinton Place
Mortensen, Mrs Margaret E, 230 E Clinton Place
Motley, Wm, colored, 417 S Fillmore ave
Motley, Mrs Ida, colored, 417 S Fillmore
Moulton, S T, land buyer, 217 E Main st
Moulton, Mrs A, 217 E Main
Moulton, Lee, 217 E Main
Mowry, Mr and Mrs, 612 S Norton ave
Muetzelfeld, Mrs Sally, 725 N Geyer ave
Muetzelfeld, Tillie, 725 N Geyer
Muldoon, John, nurseryman, 509 Collins road
Muldoon, Mrs M A, 509 Collins
Muldoon, Katie, 509 Collins
Muldoon, Mamie, 509 Collins
Muldoon, Maggie, 509 Collins
Mullen, Daniel H, clerk, cor Gill & Fillmore aves
Mullen, Daniel H J, architect, cor Gill & Fillmore
Mullen, Mrs Florence M, cor Gill & Fillmore
Mundwiller, M, maid, 505 N Taylor ave
Mungo, Mrs Vina, rear 409 S Harrison ave
Murphy, Tim, watchman Mo Pac, S Leffingwell ave
Murphy, Mrs Hanna, S Leffingwell
Murphy, Robert, tinner, S Leffingwell
Murphy, Mrs Mary, S Leffingwell
Murphy, Mrs J H, Scott & Leffingwell
Murphy, Marion, Scott & Leffingwell

Murtfeldt, Josephine, teacher, 335 E Adams ave
Murtfeldt, Mary, 335 E Adams
Murtfeldt, Augusta, 335 E Adams
Murtfeldt, Louis, 335 E Adams
Murtfeldt, Geo S, 335 E Adams
Murtfeldt, Mrs A J, 335 E Adams

OUTSIDE CITY LIMITS

McCall, Geo, Meacham Park
McCall, Mrs, Meacham Park
McCall, J G, ad writer, Parkland Place
McCall, Mrs R A, Parkland Place
McCrae, Loyd, colored, Prospect ave
McCrae, Mrs P, colored, Prospect
McDonald, I E, foreman Banner Lumber Co, N Simmons ave
McDonald, Mrs Mabel, N Simmons
McNeary, Frances, retired, N Webster ave
McNeary, Mrs G, N Webster
Misplay, John, oil wagon driver, Denny & Big Bend roads
Misplay, Mrs F, Denny & Big Bend
Moore, W S, Rollings Sporting Goods Co, Parkland Place
Moore, Mrs Mary A, Parkland Place
Morton, Mrs Mary, Parkland Place
Mueller, Mr & Mrs, Monroe & Holmes aves
Mullen, John, granitiod worker, N Simmons ave
Mullen, Mrs Della, N Simmons
Murray, John F, yard master, Parkland Place
Murray, Mrs Elizabeth, Parkland Place
Myer, Rev H M, retired, N Harrison ave
Myer, Mrs Alice, N Harrison

~ N ~

Neff, Rose, maid, 245 W Adams ave
Nelson, Miss Irene M, 155 W Main st
Neuhaus, Chas H, with Kinyon Co, S Webster ave
Neuhaus, Mrs Sarah, S Webster
Newhaus, Louis, 431 S Clay ave
Newhaus, Mrs Abbie, 431 S Clay
Newhaus, Albert, plasterer, 431 S Clay
Newhaus, Wm, driver, 431 S Clay
Newhaus, Jossie, laundry worker, 431 S Clay
Newby, Dr J B, dentist, 434 N Harrison ave
Newby, Mrs L A, 434 N Harrison
Newmann, Celia, maid, 315 S Woodlawn ave
Newton, Mack, colored, hack driver, 623 N Harrison ave
Newton, Mrs Anna, colored, 623 N Harrison
Newton, Henry, colored, carriage driver, 619 N Harrison
Newton, Mrs Bertha, 619 N Harrison
Nicolls, Samuel, Mo Lincoln Trust Co, 342 W Madison ave

Nicolls, Mrs Sarah E, 342 W Madison
Nickel, Lillian, maid, 456 N Webster ave
Nickels, Hy, carpenter, 411 W Woodbine ave
Nickels, Mrs Annie, 411 W Woodbine
Nickels, Dora, maid, 504 S Clay ave
Nieburg, J W, carpenter, 126 E Monroe ave
Nieburg, Mrs Ida, 126 E Monroe
Nimmow, George, 307 S Webster ave
Nimmow, Mrs Sarah, 307 S Webster
Nixon, Mrs F, Essex & Clay aves
Noble, P S, 245 W Adams ave
Noble, Mrs F, 245 W Adams
Nolan, Nora, servant, 345 E Main st
Nolen, Andrew, carpenter, 618 E Adams ave
North, Roso, colored, 433 W Jefferson ave
Noyes, Bradford, colored, 618 E Main st
Noyes, Mrs Ella, colored, 618 E Main st

OUTSIDE CITY LIMITS

Neader, Chas, cont concrete, 917 N Evans ave
Neader, Mrs Chas, 917 N Evans
Neeley, V E, electrician, Parkland Place
Neeley, Mrs Ethel, Parkland Place

~ O ~

Ober, E G, 212 N Woodlawn ave
Ochterbeck, Mrs Caroline, 340 E Main st
Ochterbeck, Henry C, with Victor Automobile Co, 340 E Main
Ochterbeck, Mrs Magdaline, 340 E Main
OíDonnell, P, saloon, 337 W Woodbine ave
OíDonnell, Mrs B, 337 W Woodbine
Offner, J A, Essex & Van Buren ave
Offner, Mrs Catherine, Essex & Van Buren
Offner, Mary J, Essex & Van Buren
Offner, Vincent A, Essex & Van Buren
Offner, Leo E, Essex & Van Buren
Offner, I G, Essex & Van Buren
Oge, J A, 537 N Clay
Oge, Mrs M, 537 N Clay
Oge, Richard, 537 N Clay
Olliver, David, gardner, 514 E Main st
Oliver, Mrs Clara, cook, 514 E Main st
OíMera, telegraph operator Mo Pac, 103 N Harrison ave
OíMera, Mrs Mary, 103 N Harrison
OíNeal, Claude, 444 N Van Buren ave
OíNeal, Mabel, 444 N Van Buren
Ordwein, W F, carpenter, 317 S Harrison ave
Ordwein, Mrs B, 317 S Harrison
Ormond, E W, dep mgr Carlton D G Co, S E cor Clinton & S Webster ave

Ormond, Mrs Clara G, S E cor Clinton & S Webster
Orrick, Mrs Chas, 209 W Adams ave
Orrick, Mrs Sarah T, 416 N Taylor ave
Orrick, Elizabeth B, 416 N Taylor
Orrick, Virginia P, 416 N Taylor
Osdieck, Henry, Drugs and Medicines, 201 N Webster ave, Res 113 W Jefferson ave
Osdeck, Mrs Mary, 113 W Jefferson
Ossenfort, A L, city clerk, 384 S Taylor ave
Ossenfort, Mrs L I, 384 S Taylor

OUTSIDE CITY LIMITS

OíToole, Phillip, caretaker cemetery, Big Bend road
OíToole, Mrs Delia, Big Bend
OíToole, Mrs Calla, Big Bend
OíToole, Phil Jr, Big Bend

~ P ~

Page, P W, 447 N Webster ave
Page, Mrs L G, 447 N Webster ave
Page, J C, Pac Exp Co, 507 N Clay ave
Page, Mrs Ella, 507 N Clay
Pagenstecher, R, Clothing, 117 N Webster ave, Res 121 N Webster ave
Palmer, L A, driver Polar Wave, 221 S Taylor ave
Palmer, Mrs V E, 221 S Taylor
Parker, Geo, Livery & Undertaking, 744 Cleveland ave
Parker, Mrs Celia, 744 Cleveland
Parker, Jas, colored, 403 S Harrison ave
Parker, Mrs Anne, 403 S Harrison
Parker, Mrs Martha, 334 S Fillmore ave
Parker, Mrs Martha, colored, 427 S Harrison ave
Parker, Louis, 427 S Harrison
Parker, S M, retired, 721 N Simmons ave
Parsons, Charles R, Viava Co, St Louis, 520 E Adams ave
Parsons, Mrs Anna E, 520 E Adams
Payne, Frank, 326 Rose Hill ave
Payton, Miss June, servant, 236 E Main st
Pearce, Stanley D, lawyer, 608 E Monroe ave
Pearce, Mrs O, 608 E Monroe
Pearson, M P, dentist, 446 S Clay ave
Pearson, Mrs Helen, 446 S Clay
Pendleton, Chas, with Frisco Ry, 639 N Taylor ave
Pendleton, Mrs Emma, 639 N Taylor
Perry, Bertha, servant, colored, cor Washington & Fillmore ave
Perry, R S, 312 W Jefferson ave
Perry, Mrs Ida, maid, 203 S Woodlawn ave
Peters, A, electrical engineer, 337 W Main st
Peters, Mrs G, 337 W Main
Pickel, J W, Dr, 133 E Washington ave
Pickel, Mrs L E, 133 E Washington

Pickel, Alice, 133 E Washington
Picket, Pauline, East Bodley ave
Pilgrim, Mrs E, 145 Monroe ave
Pilgrim, Lucretia, Kinloch telephone, 145 Monroe ave
Pitman & Forsythe, physicians, 207 S Webster ave
Pitman, Dr John, 316 S Webster
Pitman, Mrs E L, 316 S Webster
Polar Wave Ice & Fuel Co, Moeller mgr, Madison & Taylor
Porter, Willis, colored, 219 N Van Buren ave
Porter, Mrs Vanetta, colored, 219 N Van Buren
Porteus, Jas P, promoter, 440 N Webster ave
Potter, Rev L F, Rector Grace Church, 143 E Adams ave
Potter, Mrs Maud, 143 E Adams
Potzmann, Jos, hired man, 306 N Woodlawn ave
Powell, Mrs A R, 207 N Van Buren ave
Powell, R C, attorney, 305 N Harrison ave
Powell, Mrs A H, 305 N Harrison
Pratt, Walter E, Dupont Powder Co, 407 S Webster ave
Pratt, Mrs M E, 407 S Webster
Price, Henry, driver Holekamp, Abbett addition Mo Pac Ry
Price, Mrs M M, Abbett Addition Mo Pac Ry
Prough, D & Son, Feed and Moving, 217 and 219 Webster ave
Prough, Peter, Feed Store, 210 E Adams ave
Prough, Mrs Pauline, 210 E Adams
Purcell, W M, tinner, 331 S Webster ave
Purcell, Mrs C L, 331 S Webster
Purcell, Miss H B, clerk Post Office, 331 S Webster
Pursley, Mary, colored, 417 1/2 W Jefferson ave
Pursley, Susie, colored, 417 1/2 W Jefferson

OUTSIDE CITY LIMITS

Pearson, Howard L, engineer, Parkland Place
Pearson, Mrs L M, Parkland Place
Pfitzinger, F W, salesman Heydt Bakery, Webster ave near Manchester road
Pfitzinger, Mrs E M, Webster ave near Manchester road
Perry, Wm P, S of Big Bend road
Perry, Mrs Ida, S of Big Bend
Prough, David, retired, Big Bend
Prough, Mrs S, Big Bend
Pullis, Miss Clara, Parkland Place
Pullis, Harold, Parkland Place

~ Q ~

Quan, Frank, Bell Tel Co, 451 S Harrison ave
Quan, Mrs Ros, 451 S Harrison
Quisenberry, Edward, 358 S Taylor ave
Quisenberry, Mrs M, 358 S Taylor

Radcliff, Mrs Minnie, 517 W Washington ave
Radcliff, Celeste, 517 W Washington
Radford, Albert P, salesman, 341 E Jefferson ave
Radford, Mrs H C, 341 E Jefferson
Radford, Edgar P, salesman, 341 E Jefferson
Radford, Roy H, clerk, 341 E Jefferson
Radford, H B, with Mound City Paper Co, 128 E Jefferson
Radford, M A, 128 E Jefferson
Radotinsky, Boots & Shoes, 205 N Webster ave, Res 615 N Harrison
Radotinsky, Mrs Mary, 615 N Harrison
Reed, I A, teller Pac Exp Co, 489 N Van Buren ave
Reed, Mrs M W, 489 N Van Buren
Reed, L M, retired, 123 N Harrison
Reed, Laura, colored, 12 Santa ave
Reed, Lydia, maid, 120 E Adams ave
Reed, Wm, Mgr Electric Light Plant, 411 W Woodbine ave
Reed, Mrs Wm, 411 Woodbine
Reese, Hy, colored, concrete laborer, 460 N Geyer ave
Reese, Mrs Susie, colored, 460 N Geyer ave
Reeves, A, chauffer, 216 W Essex ave
Reeves, Mrs Ida, 216 W Essex
Reid, Mrs Anna, 429 S Harrison ave
Reid, Chas, 230 W Essex ave
Reid, Mrs Mary, 230 W Essex
Reid, Pincky, maid, 225 W Jefferson ave
Reighly, Mrs Elizabeth, 629 N Harrisonave
Renfro, Albert, colored, 425 S Geyer ave
Renfro, Mrs M, colored, 425 S Geyer
Renfro, Chas, colored, sewer digger, 413 S Fillmore ave
Renfro, Mrs Marie, colored, 413 S Fillmore
Renfro, Clark, colored, laborer, 637 E Madison ave
Renfro, Mrs Allie, colored, 637 E Madison
Renfro, Geo, colored, 353 S Fillmore ave
Renfro, Mrs L, 353 S Fillmore
Rethz, Mr & Mrs, 440 S Van Buren ave
Reveley, A L, cash Cud Pkg Co, 446 N Webster ave
Reveley, Mrs J B, 446 N Webster
Rice, Charles, colored, laborer, 125 W Main st
Rice, Geo, colored, 535 W Monroe ave
Rice, Mrs Geo, colored, 535 W Monroe
Richard, Mary, maid, Washington & Clay aves
Richter, Mrs Theodore, 527 Collins road
Ricker, E D, retired, 211 N Harrison ave
Ricker, Mrs Helen E, 211 N Harrison
Ricker, Miss Jane, 211 N Harrison
Ricker, Ira E, 211 N Harrison
Ricker, Frank H, Bank of Commerce, 522 S Clay ave
Ricker, Mrs Mary Evans, 522 S Clay

Ricker, Jake H, Bank of Commerce, 505 N Webster ave
Ricker, Mrs Mary B, 505 N Webster
Reilly, Hugh, farmer, 344 E Adams ave
Reilly, Hugh B, blacksmith, 344 E Adams
Reilly, Edward M, timekeeper U R, 344 E Adams
Reilly, Mary L, 344 E Adams
Reilly, Mrs A, 331 W Adams
Reilly, Patrick, clerk, 331 W Adams
Reilly, Mrs M, 331 W Adams
Ringcamp, Mrs J, nurse, Scott & Clark aves
Ringwalt, C L, train Aud Mo Pac, 366 S Webster ave
Ringwalt, Mrs L A, 366 S Webster ave
Ringwalt, Ralph, clerk Ind Pac Co, 414 S Clay ave
Ringwalt, Mrs Blanch, 414 S Clay
Ringwalt, Miss Ethel, 414 S Clay
Rinker, Phillip, carpenter, Menken & N Simmons ave
Rinker, Mrs Rose, Menken & N Simmons
Roark, Mrs J E, 448 N Clay ave
Roberts, Mrs Eugenia B, Scott & Holmes
Roberts, Mrs Euginia B, Scott & Holmes
Robertson, Geo F, contr plasterer, 237 S Van Buren ave
Robertson, Mrs Margaret E, 237 S Van Buren
Robinson, Mrs Susan, colored, 632 E Main st
Robinson, Emanuel, colored, 632 E Main st
Rohmier, Geo, 649 N Harrison
Robinson, Miss R G, 448 N Clay ave
Rockwell, S D, retired, 433 S Clay
Rockwell, Mrs H S, , 433 S Clay
Rode, Albert, chauffer, 516 S Webster ave
Rode, Ed, driver, 126 E Washington ave
Rode, Mrs Pauline, 126 E Washington
Roeder, Era, maid, 302 W Main st
Roemer, Lizzie, maid, 306S Webster
Rogers, A J, traveling salesman, 135 W Bodley ave
Rogers, Mrs E N B, 135 W Bodley
Rogers, Julia, 630 E Monroe ave
Rohrbach, A W, Groceries, 124 S Webster ave, Res 206 W Main st
Rollins, M, maid, Essex & Clay aves
Rosburgh, Gusta, servant, N Woodlawn ave
Ross, Jannie, colored, 337 Bouyer ave
Ross, colored, 337 Bouyer
Roth, O M, clerk Custom House, 631 N Geyer ave
Roth, Mrs Anna, 631 N Geyer
Rothweiler, Hy, clerk Feed Store, 114 W Clinton Place
Rothweiler, Mrs Emma, 114 W Clinton
Rott, Fred T, Hardware, 207 N Webster ave, Res 237 W Jefferson
Rott, Louis, Hardware Merchant, 237 W Jefferson ave
Rott, Mrs Mary, 237 W Jefferson
Ruban, Jos, laborer, 131 W Monroe ave

Ruban, Mrs Josephine, 131 W Monroe
Rubsan, Morris, stone mason, 518 N Harrison ave
Rubsan, Mrs Julia M, 518 N Harrison
Ruegg, Wm C, carpenter, 702 N Cleveland ave
Ruegg, Mrs Lena, 702 N Cleveland
Rule, H L, plasterer, 634 N Geyer road
Rule, Mrs M, 634 N Geyer
Runyan, C B, cor Washington & Fillmore aves
Rutherford, Josephine, maid, Jefferson & Fillmore
Ryan, John, conductor Mo Pac, 320 W Clinton Place
Ryan, Mrs M J, 320 W Clinton
Ryan, Wm, conductor Mo Pac, 326 W Clinton
Ryan, Mrs Susie, 326 W Clinton
Ryley, Wm, decorator, 446 S Harrison ave
Ryley, Mrs Marion J, 446 S Harrison

OUTSIDE CITY LIMITS

Rashsoe, H, Big Bend road
Rashsoe, Mrs, Big Bend
Rhodes, N, N Simmons ave
Rhodes, Mrs Mary, N Simmons
Robinson, Frank, colored, Meacham Park
Robinson, Mrs Sarah, Meacham Park
Roeder, John A, Meat Market, S Denny & New York st
Rotter, J H, Ladies Tailor, Parkland Place
Rotter, Mrs A R, Parkland Place
Rowe, D O, Buxton & Skinner, Parkland Place
Rowe, Mrs L Z, Parkland Place

~ S ~

Sakowski, I L, Tailor, 111 W Main st, Res 325 W Washington ave
Sakowski, Mrs, 325 W Washington
Sale, Mrs B H, 425 N Webster ave
Sally, Mary, maid, 209 W Adams ave
Sanders, A W, com photographer, 115 E Woodbine ave
Sanders, Mrs Clara K, 115 E Woodbine
Sanders, Andrew, colored, 511 S Geyer ave
Sanders, Jas, colored, 525 W Monroe ave
Sanders, Mrs Salli, colored, 525 W Monroe
Sandfos, John, retired, 612 N Harrison ave
Sandfos, Mrs Rossina, 612 N Harrison
Sappington, Bird T, granition contractor, 108 W Adams, Res 218 E Adams ave
Sappington, Mrs Florence, 218 E Adams
Scheetz, Miss Henrietta F, 410 N Taylor ave
Schell, Mrs C L, 120 E Adams ave
Schisler, F C, agt Merchant Life Ins Co, 527 S Clay ave
Schisler, Mrs E, 527 S Clay
Schisler, Miss Clara, 527 S Clay
Schisler, Miss Lillie, 527 S Clay

Schisler, Walter, embalmer, 527 S Clay
Schmidt, Arthur G, contractor brick work, 629 N Taylor ave
Schmidt, Mrs Matilda, 629 N Taylor
Schmidt, Oswald, bricklayer, 436 S Van Buren ave
Schmidt, Mrs J L, 436 S Van Buren
Schmitz, John, retired, Clarke & Scott aves
Schmitz, Mrs Alice, Clarke & Scott
Schmitz, John Jr, tinner, Clarke & Scott
Schmitz, Josephine, Clarke & Scott
Schnoele, J, maid, 127 W Washington ave
Schoetker, Wm, collector, Bell Tel Co, 327 W Woodbine ave
Schoetker, Mrs L, 327 W Woodbine
Schrieber, Paul, N Woodlawn
Schultz, Clara, 455 N Webster ave
Schwarzenbach, Louis, shoemaker, 431 W Main st
Schwarzenbach, Mrs Mary, 431 W Main
Schwarzenbach, E, clerk, 427 W Main
Schwarzenbach, Mrs K, 427 W Main
Scott, Mrs Ida, 201 N Van Buren ave
Searle, B L, 121 W Washington ave
Searle, Mrs J B, 121 W Washington
Seaton, G L, with Pac Exp Co, 491 Van Buren ave
Seaton, Mrs S W, 491 Van Buren
Seemann, Geo, concrete, 404 Rose Hill ave
Seemann, Mrs E L, 404 Rose Hill
Seibert, Mrs Hy, 307 S Webster ave
Seibert, Wm, carpenter, 412 Rose Hill ave
Seibert, Mrs M K, 412 Rose Hill
Seldon, J G, Union Elec L & P Co, 108 W Monroe ave
Selden, Mrs, 108 W Monroe
Selke, Miss Bertha, East Bodley ave
Shallcross, John H, 116 N Taylor ave
Shallcross, W S, Printing & Stationery, 223 S Woodlawn ave
Shallcross, Mrs L S, 223 S Woodlawn
Sharp, R O, retired, 511 S Geyer ave
Sharp, Mrs Fannie K, 511 S Geyer ave
Shaw, A F, 435 N Webster ave
Shaw, Mrs M T, 435 N Webster
Shaw, W M, stonemason, 329 E Jefferson ave
Shaw, Mrs Esther, dressmaker, 329 E Jefferson
Shaw, Isabelle, telephone, operator, 329 E Jefferson
Shaw, John, driver delivery wagon, 329 E Jefferson
Shawk, Wm, civil engineer, Leffingwell & Mo P tracks
Shawk, Mrs B, Leffingwell & Mo P tracks
Shawk, Miss Ethel, Leffingwell & Mo P tracks
Shelby, W H, Freidman Shelby Shoe Co, 514 E Main st
Shelby, Mrs P L, 514 E Main
Shelby, Lindsey, with F S Shoe Co, 514 E Main
Shelby, Miss Marian E, 514 E Main

Sherwood, F A, with Coast Products Co, 345 E Jefferson
Sherwood, Mrs Mary M, 345 E Jefferson
Shipley, J B, mfgrs Agent, 118 E Bodley ave
Shipley, Mrs I, 118 E Bodley
Shores, Mrs, colored, 220 S Geyer ave
Shores, Charles, colored, laborer, 220 S Geyer
Shuka, Wm, granitiod, 220 W Essex ave
Shuka, Mrs W, 220 W Essex
Shuka, Gilbert, 220 W Essex
Shutler, Geo, wagon maker, 114 W Madison ave
Siebecker, Emil, pressman, 215 E Washington ave
Siebecker, Mrs Emma, 215 E Washington
Siebecker, Wallace, press feeder, 215 E Washington
Siebecker, Arthur, press feeder, 215 E Washington
Silence, Mrs Martha, 307 S Webster ave
Simms, Jerry, colored, 403 S Harrison ave
Simms, Mrs Leona, 403 S Harrison
Simmons, W A, salesman, 307 N Geyer road
Simmons, Mrs, 307 N Geyer
Simmons, salesman, 307 N Geyer
Simmons, Paul, 307 N Geyer
Sing, Jim, Chinese Laundry, 141 W Main st
Sisters of St Francis, 211 W Main st

| Sr M Dosithea, | Sr M Ildephonsa, | Sr M Antonilla |
| Sr Imelda, | Sr M Louis, | Sr M Irma |

Skeele, F H, auditors office Mo Pac, 333 W Madison ave
Skeele, Mrs E B, 33 W Madison
Skeele, Miss Charlotte, 333 W Madison
Slinkard, R, Groceries, 200 N Webster ave, Res 202 N Taylor ave
Slinkard, Mrs H, 202 N Taylor
Smallwood, Susan, colored, 441 W Jefferson ave
Smith, E, Essex & Clay aves
Smith, Dr Hulbert S, dentist, 120 E Adams ave
Smith, Mrs E S, 120 E Adams
Smith, Hy, colored, 203a N Van Buren ave
Smith, Mrs Susie, 203a N Van Buren
Smith, Nola, domestic, 549 E Main st
Smith, T B, salesman, Royal Typewriter Co, 333 S Leffingwell ave
Smith, Mrs M, 333 S Leffingwell
Smith, Walter W, bank examiner, 337 W Madison ave
Smith, Mrs E T, 337 W Madison
Smith, Wm Wood, traveling salesman, 331 Way ave
Sneed, Mrs M E, 231 W Jefferson ave
Sneed, H E, 231 W Jefferson
Soehngen, Wm, saloon, 401 S Geyer ave
Soehngen, Mrs Annie, 401 S Geyer
Soehngen, Gerald, 401 S Geyer
Soeker, F, ins & notary, 430 S Geyer
Soeker, Mrs E, 430 S Geyer

Soeker, Miss Pauline, 430 S Geyer
Soeker, Mrs Johana, 430 S Geyer
Souder, Miss Daisy, teacher, Woodlawn Hotel
Spates, Mr & Mrs, Frisco & S Harrison ave
Spears, Mr and Mrs, colored, 208 Lee ave
Speckelmier, Wilmer, telegraph operator, 206 W Main
Speckert, Clara, colored, maid, 326 Clinton Place
Specking, Bernard, farmer, N Geyer ave
Specking, Mrs Annie, N Geyer
Spinner, Theo, carpenter, 124 W Clinton Place
Spinner, Mrs Emily, 124 W Clinton
Spitznagle, Ed, track walker Mo Pac, rear 202 S Taylor ave
Spitznagle, Mrs M, rear 202 S Taylor
Sprague, Frank A, Deere Plow Co, 119 E Woodbine ave
Sprague, Mrs S W, 119 E Woodbine
Sprague, Margarie, 119 E Woodbine
Sprague, Marion, 119 E Woodbine
Sprague, H E, lawyer, 544 S Clay ave
Sprague, Mrs E N, 544 S Clay
Springs, Walter, colored, 428 S Harrison ave
Springs, Mrs Nadie, colored, 428 S Harrison
Spurgeon, C A, carpenter, 329 S Clay ave
Spurgeon, Mrs A E, 329 S Clay
Spurgeon, Lee, carpenter, 329 S Clay
St John, L C, carpenter, 747 N Harrison ave
St John, Mrs Sarah, 747 N Harrison
St John, Geo, colored, Geyer & Rose Hill
St John, Mrs Susie, Geyer & Rose Hill
St Louis Express Co, Kirkwood Branch, 112 W Adams ave
St Louis National Life ins Co, 151 W Main st
Stack, Thos J, granitoid, 529 Andrews ave
Stack, Mrs L, 529 Andrews
Stanard, Frank, colored, Fillmore & Bouyer
Stanard, Mrs Elizabeth, colored, Fillmore & Bouyer
Stanley, F J, contractor & builder, 212 E Jefferson ave
Stanley, Mrs Charlotte, 212 E Jefferson
Stanley, L, driver, 212 E Jefferson
Stanley, Mabel, 212 E Jefferson
Steele, Mrs Cynthia, colored, Santa ave
Steimley, J C, plasterer, 137a S Webster ave
Steimley, Fred, plasterer, 137a S Webster
Steimley, Mrs M E, 137 a S Webster
Stemker, Rev B G, St Peters Church, 213 W Main st
Stephans, Herman, laborer, 247 Rose Hill ave
Stephans, Ed, laborer, 247 Rose Hill
Stephans, Miss A C, 247 Rose Hill
Stephans, Gast, 247 Rose Hill
Stephans, Marie, 247 Rose Hill
Steube, Wm, painter, 342 Lee ave

Steube, Mrs Elizabeth, 342 Lee
Steuber, Chas, fireman Mo Pac, Fillmore & E Monroe
Steuber, Mrs M E, Fillmore & E Monroe
Stevens, John, laborer, Woodbine & Magnolia aves
Stevens, Mrs D, Woodbine & Magnolia
Stewart, Emma, maid, 479 N Taylor ave
Still, L B, 633 N Taylor
Still, Mrs, 633 N Taylor
Stites, Mrs C, 240 E Jefferson ave
Sells, Miss Sarah, 240 E Jefferson
Stoeppelworth, Wm, carpenter, 126 E Monroe ave
Stoeppelworth, Mrs C, 126 E Monroe
Story, Leah F, colored, 205a N Van Buren ave
Straub, Chas, granitoid finisher, 418 Rose Hill ave
Straub, Mrs Margaret, 418 Rose Hill
Straub, Chris, dairyman, 446 N Geyer ave
Straub, Mrs Dora, 446 N Geyer
Straub, Fred, tinner, 335 W Woodbine ave
Straub, Mrs Augusta, 335 W Woodbine
Straub, Mrs L H, 225 S Webster ave
Straub, Chas, clerk grocer, 225 S Webster
Straub, Margaret, 225 S Webster
Straub, Louise, clerk, 225 S Webster
Stribling, Henry C, 338 W Main st
Strickland, Wm, clerk, 115 E Washington ave
Strickler, B H, Oakwood Hotel
Strohm, C, carpenter, 211 S Van Buren ave
Strohm, Mrs Carrie, 211 S Van Buren
Strohm, K F, 214 N Clay
Strohm, Miss Lee, 214 N Clay
Strohm, Miss Hailie, 214 N Clay
Strohm, Mrs Malinda, 211 S Van Buren
Strohm, Miss Fannie, 211 S Van Buren
Strus, John, retired, Fillmore & Monroe aves
Stubbs, R N, with Carleton D G Co, 212 N Woodlawn ave
Stubbs, Mrs Helen O, 212 N Woodlawn
Stubbs, Sherwood, Carlton D G Co, 212 N Woodlawn
Stuby, Wm, painter, 138 W Madison ave
Stuby, Mrs Elizabeth, 138 W Madison
Suburban Electric Co, Electric Wiring, Fixtures, 112 N Webster ave
Summers, Mrs L, 109 W Monroe ave
Summers, Julius F, 109 W Monroe
Summers, John, clerk Heege Grocery Co, 115 W Monroe
Summers, Mrs L, 115 W Monroe
Surman, Wm, granitoid contractor, 446 N Geyer ave
Surman, Mrs L, 446 N Geyer
Swan, J D, agt Trav Ins Co, 432 N Webster ave
Swan, E E, Ry man B & O, 432 N Webster
Swan, Miss Elizabeth, 432 N Webster

Swanston, Geo, 555 N Clay ave
Swanston, Mrs M J, 555 N Clay

OUTSIDE CITY LIMITS

Sackbauer, Mrs Margaret, Parkland Place
Sackbauer, Fred, clerk Mo Pac, Parkland Place
Sackbauer, Leland, clerk Mo Pac, Parkland Place
Sackbauer, Agnes, Bell Tel, Parkland Place
Sackbauer, Mary, Bell Tel, Parkland Place
Scheidegger, A J, florist, Meacham Park
Schwentker, F C, General Store, Meacham Park
Schwentker, Mrs L, Meacham Park
Sentenne, J H, Racket Store, Big Bend road
Sentenne, Mrs Olla, Big Bend road
Spears, Walter, farmer, N Evans ave
Spears, Mrs Mary, N Evans ave
Spitzenberg, C, saddler, Denny & Big Bend road
Spitzenberg, Mrs Anna, Denny & Big Bend
Spitzenberg, Miss Emma, Denny & Big Bend
Steffenns, Henry, carpenter, N Cleveland ave
Steffenns, Mrs Pauline, N Cleveland
Stewart, W E, Swift Co, Parkland Place
Stewart, Mrs Anna D, Parkland Place

~ T ~

Taylor, J P, carpenter, 743 Cleveland ave
Taylor, Mrs Annie, 743 Cleveland
Taylor, Mildred, maid, 211 N Jefferson ave
Taylor, Mrs, Woodlawn Hotel
Taylor, Miss Shelby, Woodlawn Hotel
Taylor, Mrs Margaret, colored, servant, 217 E Main st
Taussig, Mrs Edith, 549 E Main
Taussig, E A, vocal teacher, 549 E Main
Tebbetts, A, Bank of University City, Woodlawn Hotel
Tebbetts, Mrs, Woodlawn Hotel
Terry, W M, 132 W Jefferson ave
Terry, Jesse, 132 W Jefferson
Terry, C L, 132 W Jefferson
Terry, Jennie, colored, cook, 330 E Main st
Thatenhorst, Mrs C W, 402 N Webster ave
Thatenhorst, August, 402 N Webster ave
Thaxton, M C, Pac Exp Co, 229 Way ave
Thaxton, Mrs S A, 229 Way
Thaxton, Miss N A, 229 Way
Thaxton, Miss E L, 229 Way
Thoma, Mrs Louise, 238 S Van Buren ave
Thomas, Andrew, colored, laborer, 125 W Main st
Thomas, Benj F, Real Estate and Insurance, 139 S Webster ave, Res N Webster ave
Thomas, Mrs Lucy, colored, 335 S Fillmore ave

Thomas, Mary, colored, 427 S Harrison ave
Thomas, Floyd, hod carrier, 427 S Harrison
Thomas, Eugene, driver, 427 S Harrison
Thompson, F A, teamster, 118 N Geyer ave
Thomason, Mrs Aggie, 118 N Geyer
Thompson, John S, colored, 405 S Harrison ave
Thompson, Mrs Martha, 405 S Harrison
Thompson, J W, school teacher, 716 N Cleveland ave
Thompson, Mrs A K, 716 N Cleveland
Thompson, W H, carpenter, 716 N Cleveland
Thompson, Miss Lizzie, colored, 334 Lee ave
Thompson, R J, blacksmith, 139 W Main st, Res 233 W Main st
Thompson, Mrs Mary A, 233 W Main
Thompson, Miss G, stenographer, 233 W Main
Thorton, Mrs L, 207 N Van Buren ave
Thurman, P, colored, 332 W Washington ave
Thurman, Chas P, colored, 332 W Washington
Timble, Rev B N, pastor, Baptist Church, 120 E Monroe ave
Timble, Mrs A P, 120 E Monroe ave
Tompkins, Logan, banker, 415 S Webster ave
Tompkins, Mrs, 415 S Webster
Tompkins, Miss, 415 S Webster
Tompkins, W M, 435 N Webster
Tompkins, Mrs Benjamin, 435 N Webster
Tompkins, W M Jr, 435 N Webster
Tonkins, Wm R, Contractor and Builder, 203 S Taylor ave
Tonkins, Mrs E B, 203 S Taylor
Tonpkins, M M, 203 S Taylor
Townsend, Sarah, colored, 340 S Fillmore ave
Tracy, J L, pay master Cotton Belt, 504 S Clay ave
Tracy, Mrs Marion, 504 S Clay
Tracy, Miss L G, 446 N Webster
Trejbal, Mary, servant, 533 E Main st
Tremlett, Mrs J, 401 Rose Hill ave
Triggs, Mary, domestic, N E cor Essex & Webster
Troegeler, August, painter, W Madison
Troegeler, Mrs Johanna, W Madison
Troegeler, H, painter and paperhanger, Res 132 W Clinton Place
Troegeler, Mrs Emily, 132 W Clinton Place
Troegeler, Miss Mary, 718 N Dickson st
Trotter, J H, colored, teacher, 203 N Van Buren ave
Trotter, Mrs Sarah, 203 N Van Buren
Truax, J H, 109 W Jefferson ave
Truax, Mrs D, 109 W Jefferson
Tucker, A J, laborer Mo Pac, S Webster near Frisco
Tucker, Mrs U, S Webster near Frisco
Turan, Mrs colored, 419 W Jefferson ave
Turan, Drew, colored, janitor colored school, 419 W Jefferson
Turner, Albert, 669 E Madison ave

Turner, Mrs M, 669 E Madison
Turner, Mrs Betsie, colored, 661 E Madison
Turner, Ed, colored, 661 E Madison
Turner, John, colored, 427 W Jefferson ave
Turner, Mrs Georgia, colored, 427 W Jefferson
Tyler, W S, retired preacher, 143 E Clinton Place
Tyler, Mrs M E, 143 E Clinton
Tyler, Miss Lucy B, 143 E Clinton
Tyler, Rev Samuel T, colored, 421 S Harrison ave
Tyler, Mrs Mollie, 421 S Harrison

OUTSIDE CITY LIMITS

Templeton, B J, Parkland Place
Templeton, Mrs M J, Parkland Place
Templeton, Miss L, Parkland Place
Thomas, Benj F, real estate, N Webster ave
Thomas, Mrs S C, N Webster
Tiernan, H W T, Promoter, Parkland Place

~ U ~

Ude, Chas W, florist, 651 N Dickson st
Ude, F W, florist, 650 N Dickson
Ude, G A, florist, 650 N Dickson
Ude, L S M, 650 N Dickson
Ude, Mrs F, 650 N Dickson
Ude, Fred W Jr, florist, 718 N Dickson
Ude, Mrs Minnie, 718 N Dickson
Ude, Minnie, 718 N Dickson
Ude, Martin, florist, 718 N Dickson
Ulman, W A, salesman, Woodbine & Andrews aves
Ulman, Miss R, Woodbine & Andrews
Umstat, Mr & Mrs, Oakwood Hotel

~ V ~

Vallette, Alice, domestic, 479 N Taylor ave
Vandover, Claude A, farmer, 626 E Adams ave
Vandover, Lyda E, 626 E Adams
Vaughen, Geo B, ry & levy cont, 124 E Adams
Vaughan, Mrs M E, 124 E Adams
Vaughan, E B, 124 E Adams
Vaughan, Miss E P, 124 E Adams
Vernarde, Mrs L K, 127 W Washington ave
Venneman, J F, gardener, 736 N Dickson st
Venneman, Mrs C M, 736 N Dickson
Vickers, Chas E, bookkeeper, Kennard Carpet Co, 217 E Adams ave
Vickers, Mrs G H, 217 E Adams
Vickers, E Clark, 217 E Adams
Vincent, Wm, colored, 140 E Monroe ave

Vincent, Mrs Agnes, colored, 140 E Monroe
Vincent, Geo, colored, 140 E Monroe
Vincent, Mrs Mary, colored, 140 Monroe
Voigt, Julius J, tailor, 134 E Washington
Voigt, Mrs Della, 134 E Washington
Voss, Annie, maid, 111 N Harrison ave
Voss, Ida, 325 N Dickson st
Voss, Mary, maid, 112 N Harrison ave

OUTSIDE CITY LIMITS

Van Dam, Hy, telegraph operator, W Washington
Van Dam, Mrs Virginia, W Washington
Van Dam, Mise Nettie, teacher, W Washington
Van Dam, Miss, teacher, W Washington

~ W ~

Wagner, A, maid, 440 N Webster ave
Wagner, Maggie, maid, 324 N Taylor ave
Wagner, Rosalie, servant, 345 E Jefferson ave
Wagner, Ruth, domestic, 312 E Jefferson
Wahlig, Kate, maid, 503 S Webster ave
Walker, A J Rev, colored, 642 E Main st
Walker, C A, colored, Mo Pac, 439 S Clay ave
Walker, Mrs A H, 439 S Clay
Walker, Chas, colored, barber, 131 W Main st
Walker, Jefferson, 427 Rose Hill ave
Walker, Mrs, 427 Rose Hill
Walker, Kenneth, 217 E Main st
Walker, Miss Irene G, 217 E Main
Walker, Wm, colored, 327 S Fillmore ave
Walker, Mrs Jane, 327 S Fillmore
Wallace, F L, 435 N Clay ave
Wallace, Mrs M O, 435 N Clay
Wallace, Thomas, quarry man, 323 E Jefferson ave
Wallace, Mrs Mary, 323 E Jefferson
Wallace, John, tinner, 323 E Jefferson
Wallwebber, Tony, 477 S Van Buren ave
Wallwebber, Mrs F W, 477 S Van Buren
Wallwebber, Louis, hauling, 536 N Harrison ave
Wallwebber, Mrs Lena, 536 N Harrison
Walther, Rev Theodore F, Pastor Lutheran Church, 136 E Clinton Place
Walther, Mrs Marie, 136 E Clinton Pl
Walton, C C, insurance, 312 N Clay
Walton, Mrs Kate, 312 N Clay ave
Wangler, C J, Geyer and Frisco track
Wangler, Mrs F, Geyer and Frisco
Ward, F H, retired, 142 W Monroe ave
Ward, James H, Corless Chem Co, 142 W Monroe
Ward, Harry T, State Natíl Bank, 142 W Monroe

Ward, Mrs Elizabeth M, 142 W Monroe
Ward, Mrs Sarah, colored, 125 W Main st
Warfield, Mrs Lydia, 328 W Jefferson ave
Warfield, Howard M, 328 W Jefferson
Warner, George, painter, 114 W Madison ave
Warner, W F, fur merchant, 750 N Taylor ave
Warner, Mrs F G, 750 N Taylor
Warner, John B, 750 N Taylor
Warner, Wm d, fur dealer, 759 N Taylor
Warner, Mrs Estella, 759 N Taylor
Warring, E W, Furniture, 137 W Main st, Res Manchester road
Waters, Jos, colored, 325 S Fillmore ave
Watkins, Solomon, colored, 421 S Harrison ave
Watkins, Mrs Alice, colored, 421 S Harrison
Watson, Harry, mail clerk, 227 E Clinton place
Watson, Mrs Fannie, 227 E Clinton place
Watson, Jos B, colored restaurant, 127 W Main st
Way, J W, retired, 509 N Van Buren ave
Way, J Clark, 326 N Dickson
Way, C H, salesman, 326 N Dickson st
Way, Miss Mildred G, 326 N Dickson
Way, Mrs Fannie G, 326 N Dickson
Weaver, Alfred, with Kinyon Bros, S Webster ave
Weaver, John, section Mo Pac, Midway ave near Clay aves
Weaver, Mrs Rachel, Midway ave near Clay ave
Weber, Adolph, farmer, 725 N Geyer ave
Weber, J W, Groceries, etc, 138 S Webster ave, Res 339 W Woodbine ave
Weber, Mrs M, 339 W Woodbine
Weber, J F, Grocer, 4112 S Clay ave
Weber, Mrs M, 412 S Clay
Webster, H S, real estate, 208 N Webster ave,
Webster, D S, Terminal Ry, 518 S Clay ave
Webster, Mrs O C, 518 S Clay ave
Weeks, Chas, granitoid worker, 539 Andrews ave
Weeks, Mrs Elizabeth, 539 Andrews
Wagner, D, shoe cutter, S Webster near Frisco
Wagner, Otto, and Adolph, also Tillie, Lizzie, Josephine and Mrs Mary, S Webster ave near
        Frisco
Wehmeier, Mrs Kate, 335 Rose Hill ave
Wehmeier, Wm, Bell Tel Co, 335 Rose Hill
Wehmeier, Peter, carpenter, 333 Rose Hill
Wehmeier, Mrs Pluma, 333 Rose Hill
Wehmeier, Sidney, laborer, 333 Rose Hill
Wehmeier, Theodore, granitoid worker, 330 Rose Hill
Wehmeier, Mrs Maggie, 330 Rose Hill
Weichel, Matthew, gardner on Handlan place, E Main
Weichel, Mrs Rosie, E Main
Wendginsky, Andrew, shoemaker, 120 W Jefferson ave
Wendginsky, Mrs Mary, 120 W Jefferson

Wendginsky, Miss Minnie, stenographer, 120 W Jefferson
Wendginsky, Joseph, shoemaker, 120 W Jefferson
Wendginsky, Wm, painter, 120 W Jefferson
Werner, C A, 307 W Essex ave
Werner, Mrs Mary A, 307 W Essex
West, Miss Maud, teacher, 230 E Main st
Wetmore, Claud H, Washington & Clay aves
Wetmore, Mrs C, Washington & Clay
Wheeler, A J, 579 W Monroe ave
Wheeler, Mrs F S, 579 W Monroe
Wheeler, Ed, laborer, 125 W Main st
White, Benajah, real estate, Essex & Taylor aves
White, Mrs Lucy B, Essex & Taylor
White, Lucile A, Essex & Taylor
White, Mary E, Essex & Taylor
White, Morris M, Essex & Taylor
White, C W, colored, Ry man, 428 S Harrison ave
White, Mrs Clara, colored, 428 S Harrison
White, Mrs Laura, 421 N Webster ave
White, O H, com college, 221 E Jefferson ave
White, Mrs Laura S, 221 E Jefferson
Whitaker, Miss Fannie, 511 S Geyer
Whitson, H, 344 S Fillmore ave
Whitson, Mrs Daisy, 344 S Fillmore
Whyte, J G, retired, 221 W Washington
Whyte, Mrs V D, 221 W Washington
Whyte, F W, lawyer, 221 W Washington
Whyte, J Graham, dentist, 207 S Webster, Res 221 W Washtín
Wild, Fred, retired, 724 Evans ave
Wild, Mrs Louise, 724 Evans ave
Wilde, Jas B, 515 N Webster ave
Wilde, Mrs K A, 515 N Webster
Wilkinson, Norwood, colored, Woodlawn Hotel
William, Chas, barber, 115 W Main, Res N Harrison ave
Williams, E E, conductor Mo Pac, 206 N Fillmore ave
Williams, Mrs Lillian A, 206 N Fillmore
Williams, Elvia, 318 S Taylor ave
Williams, Mrs Elina, maid, 545 S Geyer ave
Williams, John, colored, Scullen & Gallagher, 316 W Clinton
Williams, Mrs Cornelia, 316 W Clinton
Williams, Mrs Mollie, colored, servant, cor Washington & Fillmore aves
Williams, Mrs M, Woodlawn Hotel
Williams, Mrs N C, 331 Way ave
Williams, N, colored, 326 Rose Hill ave
Williams, Mrs C, 326 Rose Hill
Williams, William, gardener, 603 S Geyer ave
Williams, Mrs L, 603 S Geyer
Willing Workers Home for the Aged of St Louis Co, 307 S Webster ave
Wilson, Amos, colored, 125 W Main st

Wilson, Jos N, civil engineer, 422 N Van Buren ave
Wilson, Mrs Jesse Y, 422 N Van Buren
Wilson, W G, carpenter, 429 N Clay ave
Wilson, Mrs O K, 429 N Clay
Wilson, Wm & Son, contractor & builder, 214 N Webster
Windecker, Alma, 235 E Jefferson ave
Winfrey, Claude T, 237 W Adams ave
Winfrey, Mrs Rose, 237 W Adams
Winkler, Julius, carpenter, 312 E Adams
Winkler, Mrs M, 312 E Adams
Wise, Jos, janitor, 429 E Main st
Wissman, Bertha, maid, 328 W Washington ave
Wissmann, Mrs L, 487 S Harrison ave
Wissman, Rose, house maid, 487 S Harrison ave
Wissman, Louise, house maid, 487 S Harrison
Withington, N P, 139 W Woodbine ave
Withington, Mrs E L, 139 W Woodbine ave
Wittson, Mrs L, colored, 340 S Fillmore ave
Witte, Annie, servant, 306 N Woodlawn ave
Witte, Chas, meat market, 127 S Webster ave
Wolff, M E, 143 W Jefferson ave
Wolff, J C, 143 W Jefferson
Woodlawn Inn, Mrs C W Medearis, prop, Woodlawn & Adams ave
Woods, Chas, laborer, 242 Rose Hill ave
Woods, Mrs Lillie, 242 Rose Hill
Woods, W, colored, 413 S Geyer road
Woods, Mrs Annie, colored, 413 S Geyer
Woodson, Lewis, colored, Ry E of Taylor
Woxelman, Sam, Lee ave
Woxelman, Mrs B, Lee
Wright, C A, gardener, 635 N Simmons ave
Wright, Miss E C, 635 N Simmons
Wright, Miss A E, 635 N Simmons
Wulff, G W, conductor Frisco, Geyer & Woodbine aves
Wulff, Mrs L, Geyer & Woodbine
Wyer, H G, physician & surgeon, 102a N Webster ave, Res 316 N Taylor ave
Wyer, Mrs Berenice C, 316 N Taylor

OUTSIDE CITY LIMITS

Wallbridge, J E, Wholesale drugs, Main st & Sappington rd
Wallbridge, Mrs R E, Main st & Sappington
Waters, Mrs loretta P, N W cor N Taylor & Swan aves
Weber, B R, Parkland Place
Weber, Clara M, Parkland Place
Webster, Samuel D, Geyer & Daugherty Ferry roads
Webster, Mrs A P, Geyer & Daugherty Ferry
Webster, H S, Real Estate, 208 N Webster ave, Res Geyer & Daugherty Ferry roads
Webster, F F, Geyer & Daugherty Ferry
Werth, Mrs, Sappington & Collins roads

Williams, Chas, barber, N Harrison ave
Williams, Mrs S, N Harrison
Wilson, J M, chemical works, Parkland Place
Wilson, Mrs Blance E, Parkland Place
Winter, Henry Jr, stone contractor, N Taylor ave
Winter, Mrs R L, N Taylor
Winter, Wm, florist, Taylor & Swan aves
Winter, Mrs D, Taylor & Swan
Winter, Miss Martha, Taylor & Swan
Winter, Henry, retired, Taylor & Swan
Wood, F H, Real Estate, Sappington & Suburban tracks
Wood, Mrs E, Sappington & Suburban tracks
Wood, Walter W, Painter & Paperhanger, Sappington & Suburban tracks
Wood, Frank H Jr, Maplewood Laundry, Sappington & Suburban tracks

~ Y ~

Yoder, Mrs S J, 319 W Woodbine ave
Yoder, A J, 319 W Woodbine
Young, David W, dealer in Fine Art, 323 S Webster ave
Young, Mrs M J, 323 S Webster
Young, Leigh J, 323 S Webster
Young, Miss Mary C, 323 S Webster
Young, Mrs Elizabeth, maid, N E cor Woodlawn & Monroe
Young, Fletcher W, Pac Exp Co, 315 W Adams ave
Young, Mrs Nellie C, 315 W Adams
Young, Miss Grace, teacher, 315 W Adams
Young, Frederick, 315 W Adams
Young, Ruth, 315 W Adams
Young, Ellsworth, 315 W Adams
Young, Harry, 315 W Adams
Young, H F, agent Erie Ry, 116 N Harrison ave
Young, Mrs J C, 116 N Harrison
Young, Levi, carpenter, 442 S Harrison
Young, Mrs L E, 442 S Harrison
Young, Pearl, maid, 401 S Webster ave
Yule, Alexander, 334 N Dickson st
Yule, Mrs Ann, 334 N Dickson

~ Z ~

Zampier, Ed, colored, Geyer road & Rose Hill
Zampier, Mrs Maggie, colored, Geyer & Rose Hill
Zice, Lucy, maid, 337 W Madison ave
Ziegenmeyer, Wm, carpenter, 716 N Evans ave
Ziegenmeyer, Mrs Matta, 716 N Evans
Zittlosen, Mrs Marie, 117 N Harrison ave
Zuromeste, Adam F, meter insp Suburban E L & P Co, 221 S Geyer ave
Zuromeste, Mrs L L, 221 S Geyer

STREET DIRECTORY
CITY OF KIRKWOOD

ADAMS AVE.--No. 300 north---East and West, from Geyer road to eastern city limits.

ALICE AVE.--South from Scott ave to Mo Pac Ry, 650 feet east of Clarke ave.

AMHERST AVE.--Along north side of tracks of the United Ry. Clayton division from Woodlawn ave to Parkwoods road.

ANDREWS AVE.--North and south from Woodbine to Rose Hill, 1200 feet west of Geyer.

ANGENETTE AVE.--North and south from Thomas ave to Rose Hill east of Taylor.

BODLEY AVE.--No. 500 north---East and west from Clay to Fillmore.

BOUYER LANE.--From Fillmore, 350 feet north of Clinton, west 400 feet.

CENTRAL PLACE.--From Harrison west to Van Buren, 350 feet north of Way.

CLARKE AVE.--No. 600 east---North and south from Main st to south city limits.

CLAY AVE.--No. 200 west---North and south from Rose Hill to north city limits.

CLINTON PLACE.--No. 400 south---East and west from Van Buren to Leffingwell.

COLLEGE AVE.--East and west from Webster to Clay, 350 feet north of Rose Hill ave.

COLLINS ROAD.--No. 600 north---From Woodlawn ave east to city limits.

CRESCENT DRIVE.--From Woodlawn east to Dickson, North of United Rys Clayton division.

ELLIOTT AVE.--North from south city limits to Leffingwell. thence east to east city limits

ESSEX AVE.--No. 600 north--East and west, from Taylor to west city limits.

GEYER ROAD or GEYER AVE.--No. 500 west--Northand south from limits to limits.

GILL AVE.--East and west from Fillmore to Woodlawn, 660 feet north of Adams.

GRAND AVE.--East and west from Webster to Harrison along north side of Frisco Ry.

HARRISON AVE.--No. 300 west---North and south from limits to limits.

HAWBROOK ROAD --From Dickson, 850 feet north of Adams, east to Parkwoods Road.

HEEGE AVE.--East and west from Harrison to Van Buren, 180 feet north of Woodbine.

HILLCREST PLACE --Begins at Woodbine, 380 feet west of Clay, running north 300 feet.

IDLEWILD AVE.--East and west, from Wabster to Clay, 350 feet south of Woodbine.

JEFFERSON AVE.--No. 200 north--East and west, from Geyer to Smith ave., and from Woodlawn to 566 feet east of Dickson.

LEE AVE.-East and west from Harrison to Geyer, 350 feet north of Rose Hill.

LEFFINGWELL AVE.--No. 400 east-- South from Mo. Pac. Ry. to Elliot, thence southeast to city limits.

LILLIAN AVE.--East and west, from Fillmore to Elliot, south of Woodbine.

MADISON AVE.--No. 200 south--East and west from Geyer to Harrison and from Clay to east city limits.

MAGNOLIA AVE.--From Rose Hill ave. 458 feet west of Geyer, north to Mo. Pac. Ry. 614 feet west of Geyer.

MAIN STREET--dividing line for streets running north and south, numbers beginning with No. 100 on each side--Runs east and west from limits to limits.

McKINLEY AVE.--From Magnolia, 300 feet north of Woodbine, to west city limits.

MIDWAY AVE.--East and west from Minnie ave. to Harrison ave.,300 feet south of Rose Hill ave.

MINNIE AVE.--Beginning at Grand ave. 400 feet west of Webster, running north 350 feet.

MONROE AVE.--No. 300 South--East and west from limits to limits.

NIRK AVE.--East and west from Geyer to Magnolia, 750 feet north of Woodbine.

NORTON AVE.--North andsouth, from Lillian to south city limits, east of Fillmore.

RAILROAD STREET--West on south side of Mo. Pac. Ry. from Webster to Clay. West on south side of Mo. Pac. Ry. from near Harrison to Geyer. Also east on south side of Mo. Pac. Ry. from Webster to Taylor and from Fillmore to east city limits. Also on north side _____of Mo. Pac. Ry. from Fillmore to east city limits.

CLEVELAND AVE.--No. 400 west---North and south from Essex to north city limits.

DICKSON STREET.--No. 600 East---North and south, from Main street to north city limits.

EVANS AVE.--North and south, from Essex to north city limits. Next west of Harrison.

FILLMORE AVE.--No.300 east---North and south, from Essex to south city limits.

GILBERT ST.--North and south, from Main to Madison, 300 feet east of Fillmore.

HOLMES AVE.--East city limits, from Main street to south city limits.

JEWEL AVE.--East and west, from Webster to Clay, north of Essex.

MENKENS AVE.--No. 700 north---East and west, from Harrison to Geyer.

MERMOD BL.--East to west, from Webster to Clay, north of Essex

MIRIAM AVE.--North and south, from Scott to Mo Pac Ry, 320 feet east of Clarke.

PARKWOODS ROAD--From Adams ave, 300 feet east of Dickson, north to Collins road.

PEAKE AVE.--North city limits, from Webster west to Geyer.

PEARL AVE.--From Essex, 280 feet east of Harrison, north 800 feet.

ROSE HILL AVE.--No. 600 south---East and west, from Fillmore to west city limits.

SANTA AVE.--Begins at Fillmore 550 feet south of Monroe, running east 360 feet.

SCHWEN AVE.--East and west along north side Frisco Ry, from Fillmore to Elliott.

SOUTH TAYLOR--Running from Thomas ave south 340 feet.

SIMMONS AVE.--North and south, from Essex to north city limits. next west of Cleveland.

SMITH AVE.--No.400 east---North and south, from Main st to Mo Pac Ry.

SWAN AVE.--North city limits, from Webster east to Taylor.

TAYLOR AVE.--No. 200 east---North and south from Woodbine to north limits.

THOMAS ST.--No. 700 north---From Webster east to Taylor.

VAN BUREN AVE.--No.400 west---North and south from Woodbine to Essex.

WASHINGTON AVE.--No. 400 north---East and west, from Fillmore to west city limits.

WAY AVE.--No. 500 north---East and west, from Clay to Geyer.

WEBSTER AVE.--Dividing line for streets running east and west, numbers beginning with No. 100 on each side--Runs north and south from limits to limits.

WOLVERTON AVE.--From Magnolia, 750 feet north of Woodbine, to west city limits.

WOODLAWN AVE.--No. 500 east---North and south, from Mo Pac Ry to north city limits.

WOODBINE AVE.--No. 500 south---East and west, from Fillmore to west city limits.

———

Time Tables and Routes of Street Car Lines

———

United Railways Manchester Division.

———

TIME TABLE

EAST BOUND--First car leaves Geyer Road at 5:45 a. m. and cars then run every 15 minutes until about 1:30 a. m.

WEST BOUND--First car leaves Maplewood at 5:20 a. m. Cars then run every 15 minutes until midnight, the last car leaving Fourth and Elm streets, St. Louis, at 12 midnight, arriving in Kirkwood at 1:15.

ROUTE OF TRACKS

WEST BOUND--Enters Kirkwood on Adams ave. at Eastern city limits; continues east on Adams, crossing Dickson st, Woodlawn ave. Smith stop, to Fillmore ave.: thence north on Fillmore one block to Washington; thence West on Washington, crossing Taylor ave., Webster ave. to Clay ave.; thence south on Clay, crossing Adams ave., Jefferson ave., Main st., Madison ave., Monroe ave., W Clinton Place west of Clay, W. Clinton Place east of Clay to woodbine ave.; thence west on Woodbine, crossing Hillcrest Place, Harrison ave., Van Buren ave., Geyer road, Magnolia ave., Andrews ave., western city limits.

EAST BOUND--Enters Kirkwood on Woodbine at western city limits: continues east on Woodbine, crossing Andrews ave.,Magnolia ave., Geyer road, Van Buren ave., Harrison ave., Hillcrest Place, to Clay ave.; thence north on Clay, crossing W. Clinton Place east of Clay, W. Clinton Place west of Clay, Monroe ave., Madison ave., Main street, Jefferson ave., to Adams ave.; thence east on Adams ave., crossing Webster ave., Taylor ave., Fillmore ave., Smith stop, Woodlawn ave., Dickson street, eastern city limits.

United Railways Kirkwood-Ferguson Division

TIME TABLE

SOUTH BOUND--First car leaves DeHodiamont 5:00 a.m. Second car leaves at 5:30 a.m. and cars then run every 20 minutes until midnight, the last leaving DeHodiamont 12:10 a.m.

NORTH BOUND--First car leaves Kirkwood at 5:50 a.m. Second car leaves at 6:20 and cars then run every twenty minutes until 1 a.m., when the last car leaves Kirkwood.

ROUTE OF TRACKS

SOUTH BOUND--Enters Kirkwood over private right of way at northeastern city limits; continuing it crosses Parkwoods road, Dickson street, Woodlawn ave., to Fillmore ave.; thence south on Filmore, to Washington ave., crossing Gill ave.; thence west on Washington, crossing Taylor ave., Webster ave., to Clay ave.; thence south on Clay, crossing Adams ave., Jefferson ave., to Main street, where transfers are given to Manchester Division for further points south and west.

NORTH BOUND--Leaving Main street, Kirkwood, cars run north on Clay ave., crossing Jefferson ave., to Adams ave.; thence east on Adams, crossing Webster ave., Taylor ave., to Fillmore ave.; thence north on Fillmore, crossing Washington ave., Gill ave., to private right of way, thence east on private right of way, crossing Woodlawn ave., Dickson street, Parkwoods road, northeastern city limits.

"African American Military Roles" http://www.autositecreator.com/websites/10685/1.htm

Kirkwood Celebration. pp. 28, 72-74. 1990

Kirkwood Historical Review, Vol. 4, No. 3, September 1965.

Kirkwood Historical Review, Vol. 4, No. 4, December 1965.

Chomeau, Mary Broderick. Some Early Negro Families of Kirkwood.

Beck, Betty. Kirkwood Highlights. 1978

Kirkwood Facts About Your Hometown, 1940

Historic Kirkwood Landmarks, p. 26. October 2001.

Early Kirkwood, Volume 11, 1988

Fox, Tim. Where We Live. pp. 174-178. 1995

Speer, Lonnie R. A Brief History of Mecham Park, Mo. 1998

Kremer, Gary R. Missouri's Black Heritage. 1993

Thompson, Chris. Directory of the City of Kirkwood. 1910

St. Louis Recorder of Deeds. Book 8074, p. 223

Kirkwood City Ordinance #6303

Missouri Veterans Communications, Carl A. Hargus

DAR Missouri East Central Cemetery Records, Vol. 1 Salt Lake City, SOC, Utah, 1994. FHL
        Film OQ62589:3

Dahl, Jane. A Brief History of Kirkwood Missouri, 1851-1965

DAR Missouri John Sappington Chapter East Central Missouri Cemetery Records NP 1994.
        Type Script FAR. History. Library. Salt Lake City.

St. Louis Recorder of Deeds. Book 320 p. 315

Green, Robert Ewell. The Way We Were. pp. 264-166. 1993

Kirkwood Olive Chapel and AME Church. Norma J. Rhodes

Wright, John A. <u>Discovering African Americans.</u> St. Louis, Mo., 1994

Louerde, Mary. <u>Touching Tomorrow.</u> 2002

Amsler, Kevin. <u>Final Resting Place.</u> 1997

Avery, John D. <u>Funeral Practices of the Late 1800's & Early 1900's.</u> St. Louis, MO., 2002

Friends of Father Dickson Cemetery
St. Peters Catholic Cemetery
Oak Hill Cemetery

The Association for Gravestone Studies

Jay B. Smith Funeral Home
Ortmann Funeral Home
Baue Funeral Home
Buchholz Mortuariea Inc
Schnur Funeral Home
John E Hallmark Funeral Service Co.
John L. Ziegenhein and Sons Funeral Home
Ualhall Chapel
Bopp Chapel
Schumacher Chapel
Pfitzinger Mortuary
Ted Yandell Mortuary
Wade Funeral Home
St. Louis Post Dispatch, Phil Sutin, May 2002
St. Louis Post Dispatch, Marianna Riley, March 1980
Nation Trust For Historic Preservation, Lynette Strangstad
Kirkwood Public Library
St. Louis County Library
St. Louis Genealogical Society
Kirkwood Historical Society Library
West Post, April 9, 2001
National Personal Records Center
Millitary Records
State Laws Regarding Cemeteries, Missouri State 194.410, 214.041, 214.131, 214.205.2,
     214.205.6
Missouri State Archives, Denise Ziegeiben
National Archives and Records, Cynthinia G. Fox, Chief, Old Military and Civil Records
Textual   Archives Service Division.
Department of Natural Resources
Webster-Kirkwood Times, April 2002, July 19, 1998, November 1986, April 19, 2001, July 2001
Veteran Affairs National Cemetery Administration, De Anna L. Wilson, Chief of
     Communications Regulatory Division

Frank X. Muehlbauer, c. November 1969
Isabel Stebbins Giulvezan, c. November 1969
Morris, Ann. <u>A Grave Undertaking</u>. 2002
Robert Ewell Green
Erma J. Reed
Reverend Brenda J. Hayes
Louis H. Bopp II
Christine Bopp
Richard C. Mueller Jr.
Bertha Madilene Spears Evans
Emmett Benson
Audrey Grimes
George C. Davis III
Michael Whitson
Joe Cole
Lorraine Brown
Marian Willis Cutts
William N. St. James
Patricia McKissack
Richard James
Marion Brooks
Ann Morris
Carolyn Altepcter
William L. Slaten
Malcolm Button
Bill Pfitzinger
Harold Whitfield

Photograph Credits

1860's Horse Drawn Hearse Photo by Permission of
Cher Petrovic
6519 Cherokee
Cedar Hill, MO 63016

Casket reprints by permission of
Museum Of Funeral Customs
1440 Monument Ave.
Springfield, IL 62702

Coffin Litho reprint by permission of
Criswell Casket Company
St. Louis, Missouri

communications
St. Louis